Baby Quilts

Susan Emory

LEISURE ARTS, INC. • Maumelle, Arkansas

The anticipation of a new baby is the perfect inspiration for a handmade gift and the best gifts to give are created by you.

With simple piecing and basic appliqué these baby quilts are styled for today's creative baby room. There is something sweet and soft about baby quilts and the fabric that goes into them. Indulge yourself with modern fabric choices and the process of making these very special quilts. This book includes seven baby quilt patterns and a variety of styles to provide a meaningful handmade gift.

Susan Emory

Quilting is a long-standing tradition in Susan Emory's family. She is a fifth generation quilter and turned her hobby into a business when she bought a quilt shop in 2006. As a graphic designer, Susan was inspired to design quilts and formed Swirly Girls Design in 2008.

In addition to quilt patterns and books, Susan is a licensed designer for Michael Miller Fabrics, Dill Buttons and Creative Grids™. She eventually sold her quilt shop to focus on design and teaching.

Susan is actively involved in the quilting industry, a member of the International Association of Creative Arts Professionals, a member of Central Virginia Modern Quilt Guild, and an Aurifil™ Thread Specialist.

When not traveling and teaching, she lives at home with her husband, Mike, in Moseley, Virginia. They have three adult children Muriah, Alyssa, and Chance.

To see Susan's latest fabric lines and for more creative motivation visit www.swirlygirlsdesign.com.

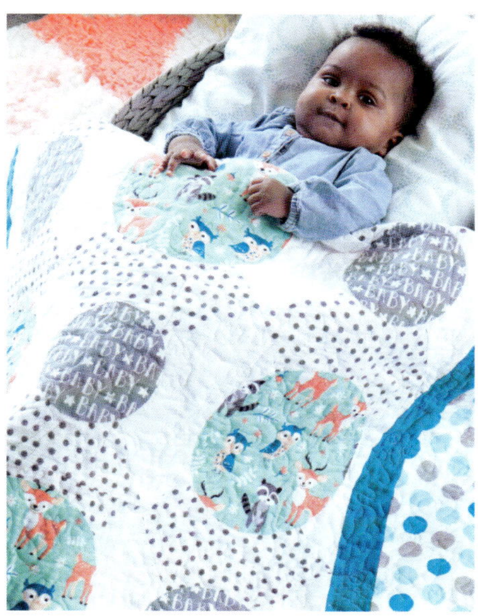

OH BABY

Express yourself using solids or prints in this chic design.

SHOPPING LIST

Yardage is based on 43"/44" wide fabric with a usable width of 40".

- ☐ 2³/₄ yds of solid white fabric for background
- ☐ ¹/₂ yd ***each*** of 6 solid color fabrics
- ☐ 3³/₈ yds of fabric for backing
- ☐ ¹/₂ yd of fabric for binding

You will also need:

- ☐ 6¹/₂ yds of 17" wide paper-backed fusible web
- ☐ 56" x 60" piece of batting
- ☐ Creative Grids™ Circle Savvy Ruler (optional)
- ☐ template plastic and permanent marker (optional)

Finished Quilt Size: 48" x 52"

CUTTING THE PIECES

*Follow **Rotary Cutting**, page 39, to cut fabric. WOF = cut strips across width of fabric from selvage to selvage. All measurements include ¹/₄" seam allowances.*

From solid white fabric for background:

- Cut [20] 4¹/₂" x WOF strips; from these strips, cut [156] 4¹/₂" squares.

From *each* of 6 solid color fabrics:

- Cut [3] 4¹/₂" x WOF strips; from these strips, cut [24] 4¹/₂" squares.

From fabric for binding:

- Cut [6] 2¹/₂" x WOF strips.

From paper-backed fusible web:

- Cut [144] 4¹/₂" squares.

MAKING THE BLOCKS

*Follow **Machine Piecing** and **Pressing**, page 40, to make quilt top. Use $^{1}/_{4}$" seam allowances throughout. I recommend the Creative Grids™ Circle Savvy Ruler for cutting perfect circles but you may use the quarter-circle pattern, page 7, instead.*

1. Set aside [12] $4^{1}/_{2}$" white background squares. These squares will not be fused or cut.

2. Following fusible web manufacturer's instructions, center and fuse [1] $4^{1}/_{2}$" square of fusible web to the wrong side of [72] white background squares and [12] of each color of $4^{1}/_{2}$" squares.

3. Align the SEAM ALLOWANCE lines marked on the Creative Grids™ Circle Savvy Ruler with the bottom and left edges of a fused square. Cut the arc using the 8" slot on the ruler to make a quarter-circle **(Fig. 1)**. Repeat with the remaining fused white background squares and fused color squares.

4. Fuse a white background quarter-circle to [12] of each color of $4^{1}/_{2}$"square, aligning the bottom and left edges **(Fig. 2)**. Stitch around the arc using the appliqué stitch of your choice. I recommend Edge Stitch, Blanket Stitch, Zig Zag Stitch, or Satin Stitch.

5. Repeat Step 4 to fuse a color quarter-circle to each of [72] $4^{1}/_{2}$" white background squares, aligning the bottom and left edges **(Fig. 3)**. Stitch around the arc using the appliqué stitch of your choice.

Fig. 1

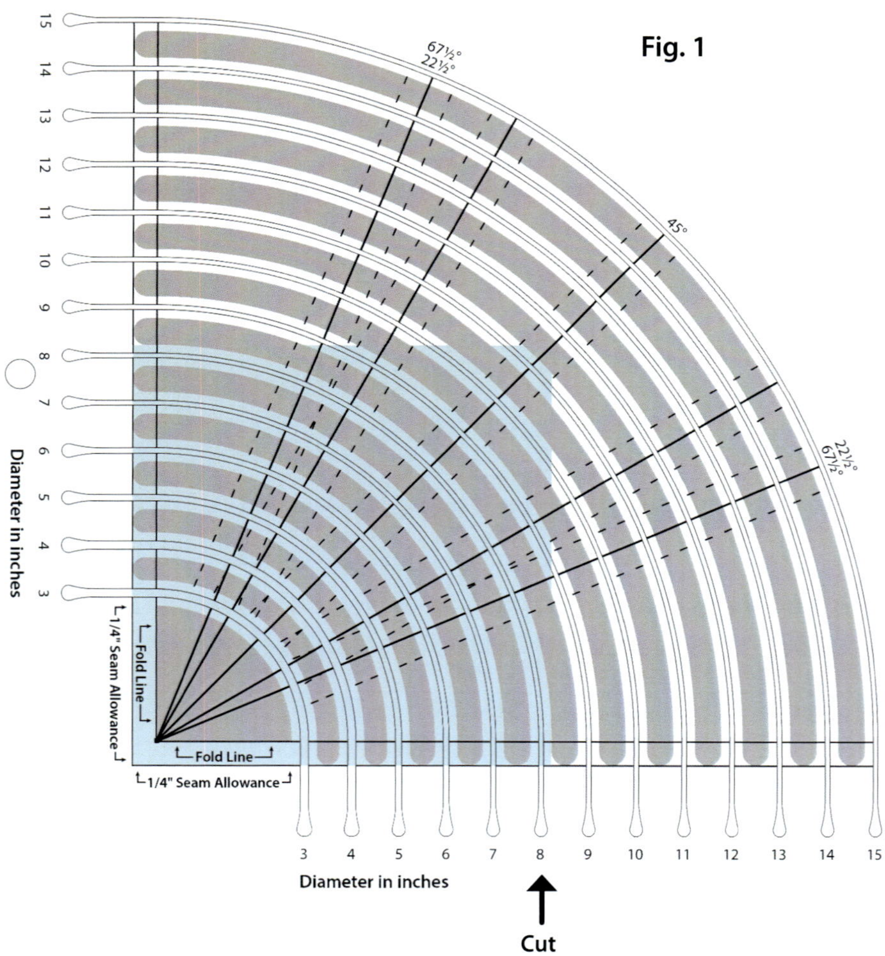

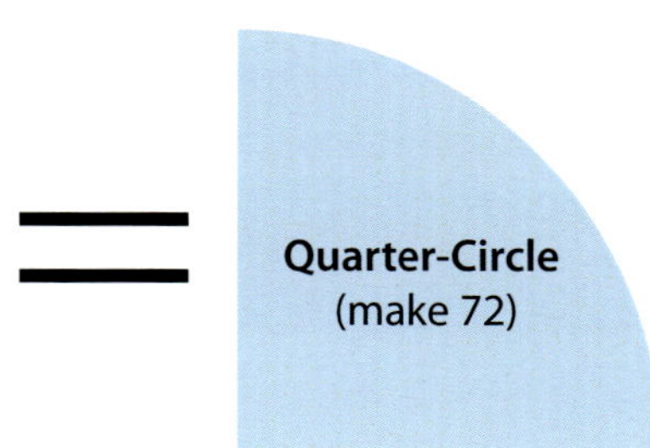

Note: For **Fig. 1**, white fabric is shown in blue for clarity.

Fig. 2

Fig. 3

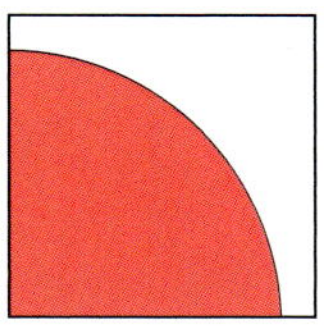

Quilt Top

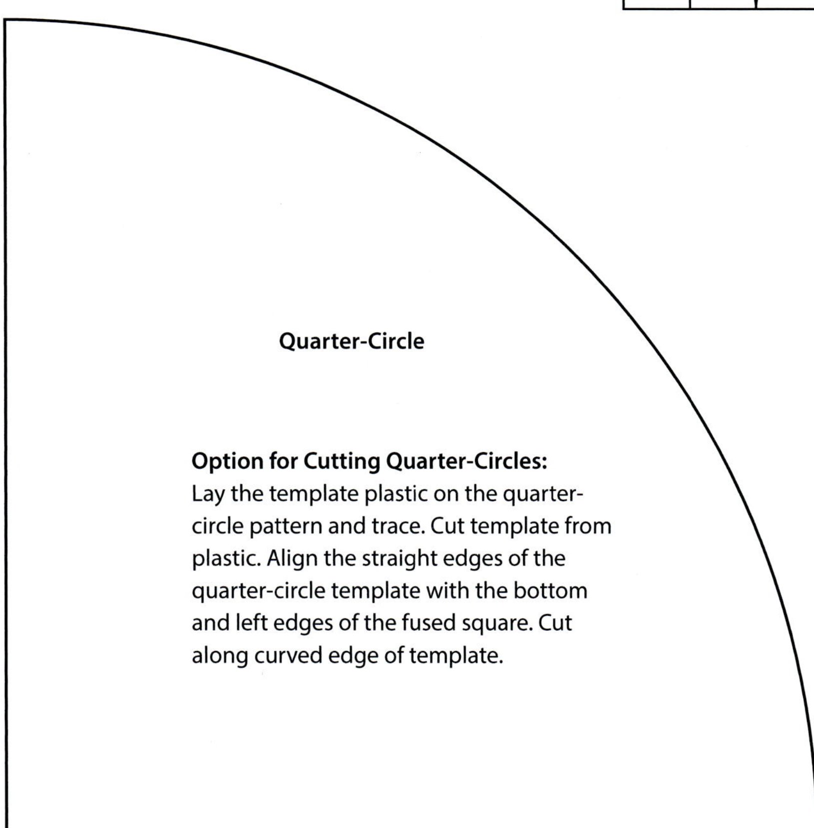

Option for Cutting Quarter-Circles:
Lay the template plastic on the quarter-circle pattern and trace. Cut template from plastic. Align the straight edges of the quarter-circle template with the bottom and left edges of the fused square. Cut along curved edge of template.

ASSEMBLING THE QUILT TOP

*Refer to **Quilt Top** for assembly.*

1. Arrange all units and squares as shown. Sew blocks together into horizontal rows and press. Sew rows together and press to complete **Quilt Top**.

COMPLETING THE QUILT

1. Follow **Quilting**, page 43, to mark, layer, and quilt as desired. Quilt shown is quilted with a different pattern in each background and colored area.

2. Follow **Making a Hanging Sleeve**, page 45, if a hanging sleeve is desired.

3. Use **binding strips** and follow **Making Straight-Grain Binding**, page 45, to make binding. Follow **Attaching Binding with Mitered Corners**, page 46, to bind quilt.

ALL ABOARD

Wrap your sweet baby in warmth using bright prints and a flannel border.

SHOPPING LIST

Yardage is based on 43"/44" wide fabric with a usable width of 40". Fat quarters are approximately 22" x 18".

- ☐ fat quarter ***each*** of 8 assorted prints and solids
- ☐ 1 1/4 yds of white fabric for background
- ☐ 3/4 yd of fabric for border
- ☐ 3 5/8 yds of fabric for backing
- ☐ 3/4 yd of fabric for binding

You will also need:

- ☐ 56" x 64" piece of batting

Finished Quilt Size: 48" x 56"

CUTTING THE PIECES

*Follow **Rotary Cutting**, page 39, to cut fabric. WOF = width of fabric from selvage to selvage. For fat quarters, cut strips parallel to the long edge. Border is cut exact length. All measurements include 1/4" seam allowances.*

From *each* of 8 fat quarters:

- Cut [8] 5" squares.

From background fabric:

- Cut [8] 5" x WOF strip; from these strips, cut [60] 5" squares.

From fabric for border:

- Cut [5] 4 1/2" x WOF strips.

From fabric for binding:

- Cut [1] 25" square.

ASSEMBLING THE QUILT TOP

*Follow **Machine Piecing** and **Pressing**, page 40, to make quilt top. Refer to **Quilt Top** for assembly. Use $^1/_4$" seam allowances throughout.*

1. Draw a diagonal line on the wrong side of [60] 5" background squares. With right sides together, place a 5" background square on top of a 5" print square. Stitch $^1/_4$" on each side of drawn line **(Fig. 1)**. Cut along drawn line **(Fig. 2)** and press toward darker fabric to make a **Half-Square Triangle**. Trim half-square triangle to $4^1/_2$" square. Repeat with remaining 5" squares to yield a total of [120] half-square triangles. ***Note:*** *You will have [4] extra 5" print squares.*

2. Arrange all half-square triangles as shown in **Fig. 3**; rearrange as desired to balance colors. Sew together in horizontal rows. Press each row of blocks in the opposite direction from the row before. Sew rows together and press to complete **Quilt Top Center**.

3. Trim selvages from [5] $4^1/_2$" x WOF border strips and sew together end to end.

4. Cut [4] strips $48^1/_2$" long. Sew a border to each side of quilt. Press toward border strips.

5. Sew a border to top and bottom of quilt. Press toward border strips to complete **Quilt Top**.

Fig. 1

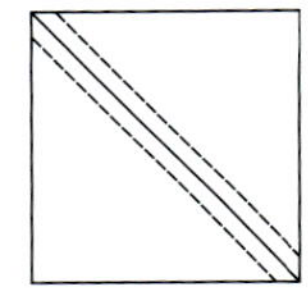

Fig. 2

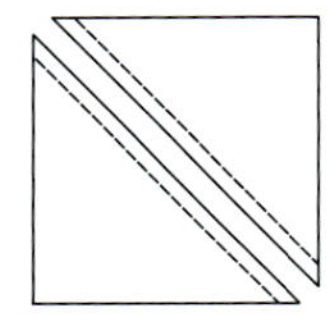

Half-Square Triangle (make 120)

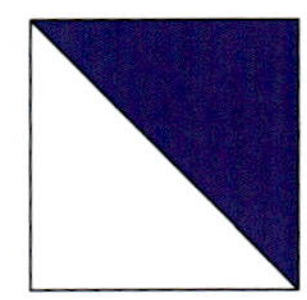

Fig. 3

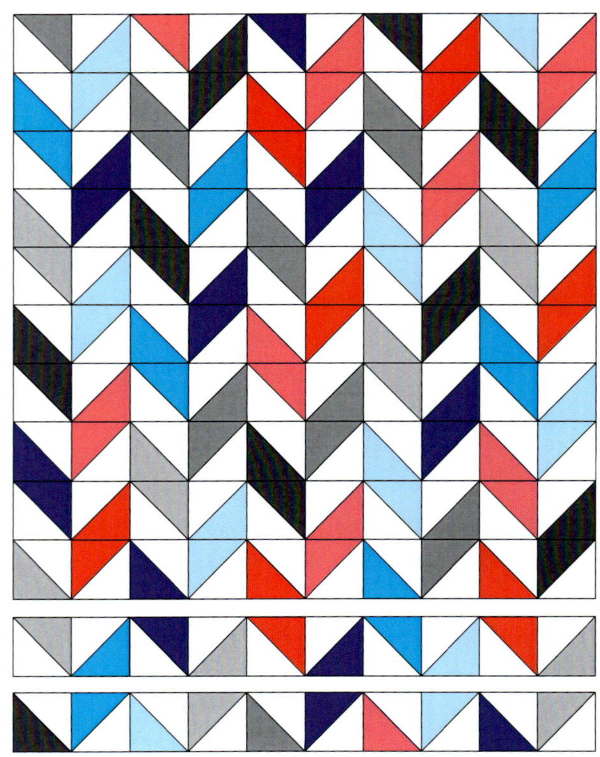

COMPLETING THE QUILT

1. Follow **Quilting**, page 43, to mark, layer, and quilt as desired. Quilt shown is quilted with an allover wave pattern with randomly spaced anchors.

2. Follow **Making a Hanging Sleeve**, page 45, if a hanging sleeve is desired.

3. Use **square** and follow **Making Continuous Bias Binding**, page 45, to make binding. Follow **Attaching Binding with Mitered Corners**, page 46, to bind quilt.

Quilt Top Center

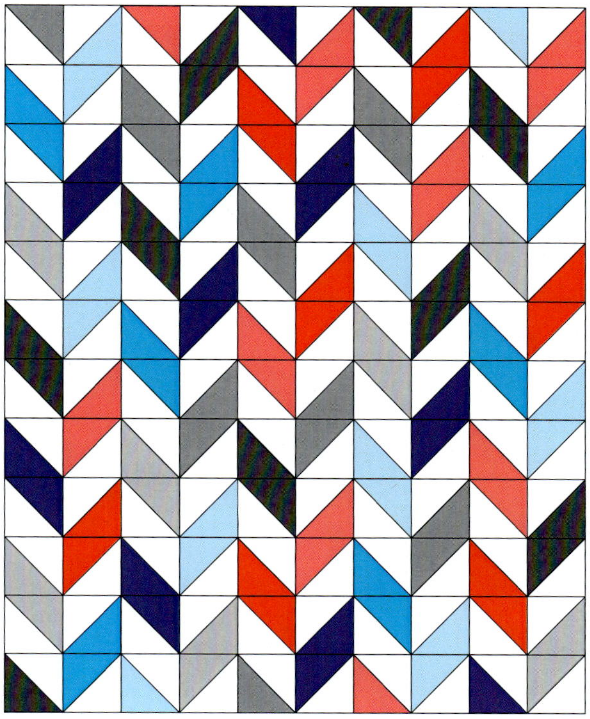

Quilt Top

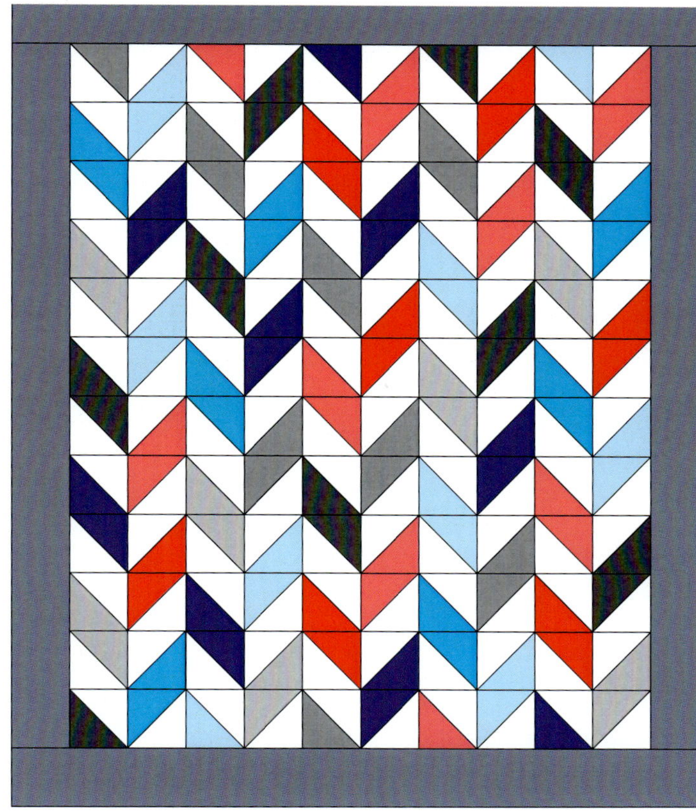

SIGNING & DATING YOUR QUILT

A completed quilt is a work of art and should be signed and dated. There are many different ways to do this and numerous books on the subject. The label should reflect the style of the quilt, the occasion or person for which it was made, and the quilter's own particular talents. The following are suggestions for recording the history of the quilt or adding a sentiment for future generations.

- Embroider quilter's name, date, and any additional information on quilt top or backing. Matching floss, such as cream floss on white border, will leave a subtle record. Bright or contrasting floss will make the information stand out.
- Make label from muslin and use permanent marker to write information. Use different colored permanent markers to make label more decorative. Stitch label to back of quilt.
- Use photo-transfer paper to add image to a white or cream fabric label. Stitch label to back of quilt.
- Piece an extra block from quilt top pattern to use as label. Add the information with a permanent fabric pen. Appliqué block to back of quilt.
- Write message on appliquéd design from quilt top. Attach appliqué to back of the quilt.

CIRCUS ACT

Use a sweet novelty print as the focal point of your blocks.

SHOPPING LIST

Yardage is based on 43"/44" wide fabric with a usable width of 40".

- ☐ 1/2 yd of elephant print fabric for Block A center squares
- ☐ 1/2 yd of solid white fabric for Block A triangles
- ☐ 1/2 yd ***each*** of 4 print fabrics for Block A frames
- ☐ 3/8 yd of print fabric for Block B center squares
- ☐ 7/8 yd of solid gray fabric for Block B frames
- ☐ 7/8 yd of polka dot fabric for setting triangles
- ☐ 3 5/8 yds of fabric for backing
- ☐ 1/2 yd of fabric for binding

You will also need:

- ☐ 53" x 65" piece of batting

Finished Quilt Size: 45" x 57"
Finished Block Size: 8" x 8"

CUTTING THE PIECES

*Follow **Rotary Cutting**, page 39, to cut fabric. WOF = cut strips across width of fabric from selvage to selvage. All measurements include $^{1}/_{4}$" seam allowances.*

From elephant print fabric for Block A center squares:

- Cut [3] 4$^{1}/_{2}$" x WOF strip; from these strips, cut [20] 4$^{1}/_{2}$" squares.

From solid white fabric for Block A triangles:

- Cut [5] 2$^{1}/_{2}$" x WOF strip; from these strips, cut [80] 2$^{1}/_{2}$" squares.

From *each* of 4 print fabrics for Block A frames:

- Cut [1] 8$^{1}/_{2}$" x WOF strip; from this strip, cut [10] 2$^{1}/_{2}$" x 8$^{1}/_{2}$" rectangles.
- Cut [1] 4$^{1}/_{2}$" x WOF strip; from this strip, cut [10] 2$^{1}/_{2}$" x 4$^{1}/_{2}$" rectangles.

From print fabric for Block B center squares:

- Cut [2] 4$^{1}/_{2}$" x WOF strips; from these strips, cut [12] 4$^{1}/_{2}$" squares.

From solid gray fabric for Block B frames:

- Cut [2] 8$^{1}/_{2}$" x WOF strip; from these strips, cut [24] 2$^{1}/_{2}$" x 8$^{1}/_{2}$" rectangles.
- Cut [2] 4$^{1}/_{2}$" x WOF strip; from these strips, cut [24] 2$^{1}/_{2}$" x 4$^{1}/_{2}$" rectangles.

From polka dot fabric for setting triangles:

- Cut [2] 12$^{1}/_{2}$" x WOF strips; from these strips, cut [4] 12$^{1}/_{2}$" squares. Cut each square twice diagonally to make 16 large setting triangles. From remainder of strips, cut [2] 6$^{1}/_{2}$" square. Cut these squares once diagonally to make 4 small setting triangles.

From fabric for binding:

- Cut [6] 2$^{1}/_{2}$" x WOF strips.

Fig. 1

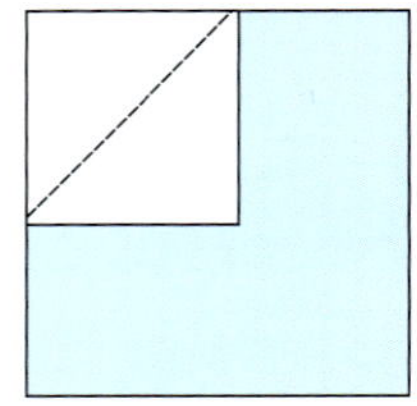

Fig. 2

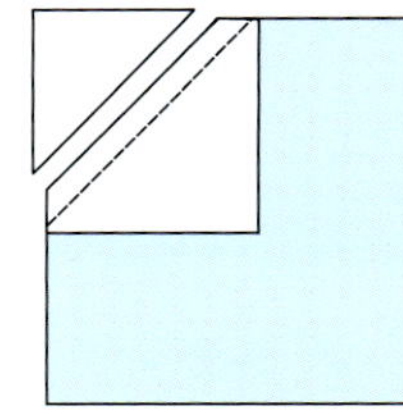

Fig. 3

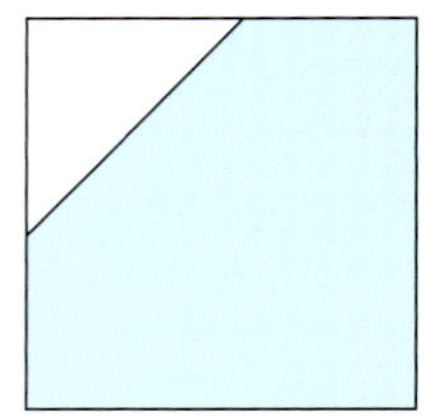

Square-in-a-Square Unit
(make 20)

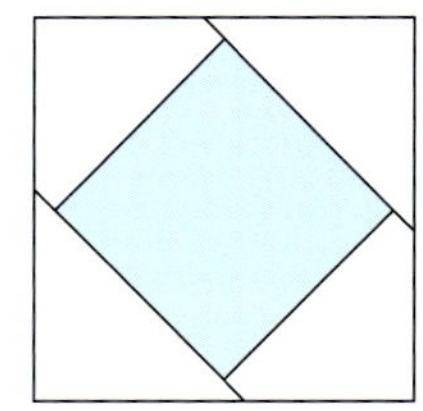

Block A
(make 20)

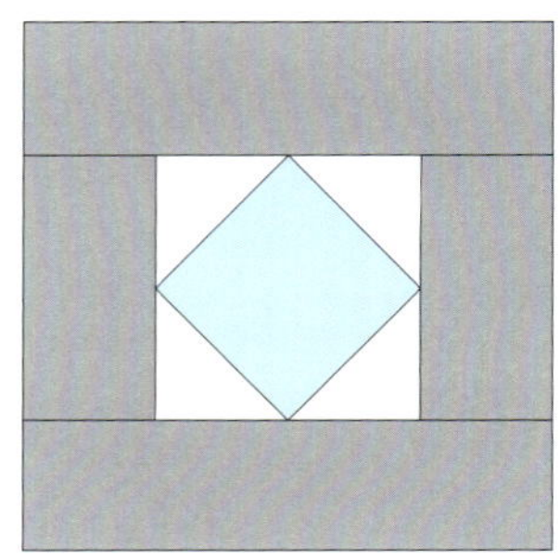

Fig. 4

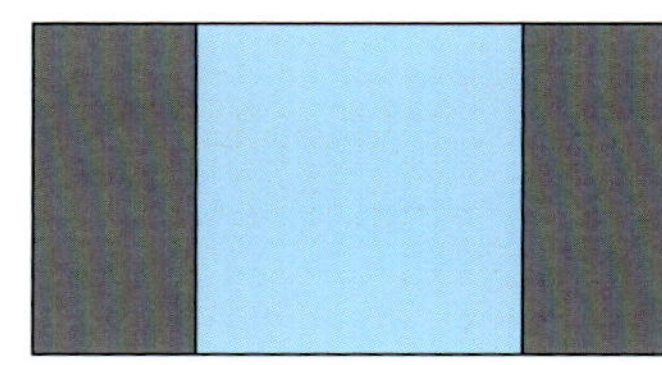

Block B
(make 12)

Fig. 5

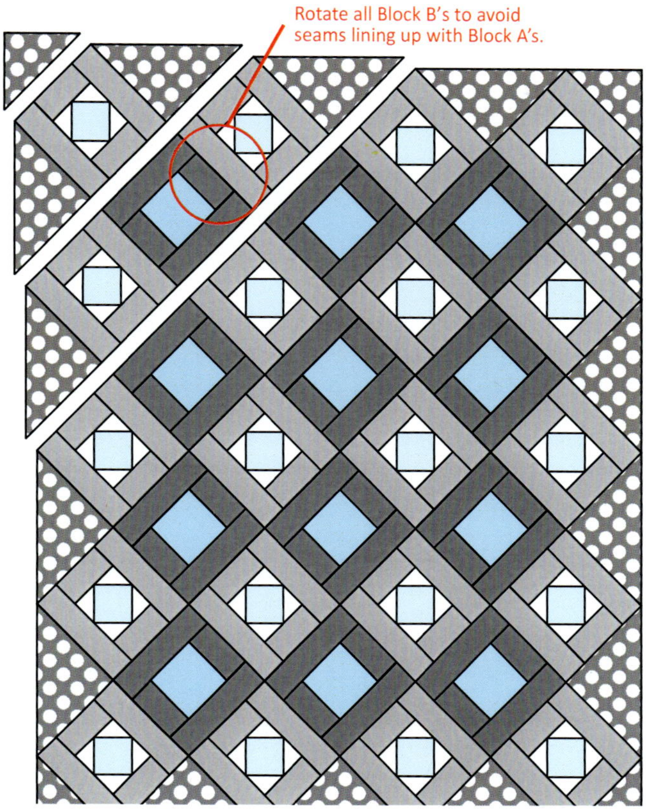

Quilt Top

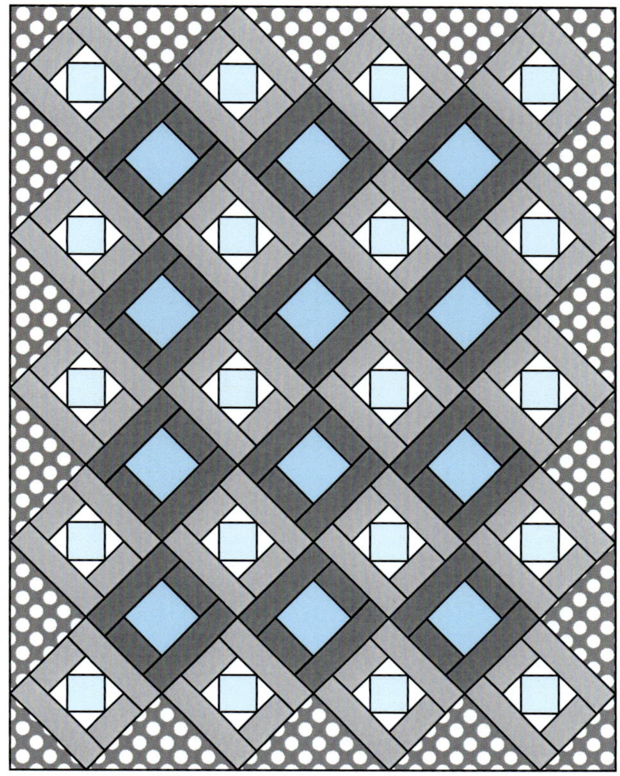

MAKING THE BLOCKS

*Follow **Machine Piecing** and **Pressing**, page 40, to make quilt top. Use 1/4" seam allowances throughout.*

1. Draw a diagonal line from corner to corner on the wrong side of [80] 2 1/2" Block A squares. With right sides together, place a 2 1/2" square on one corner of a 4 1/2" Block A center square **(Fig. 1)**. Stitch on the drawn line. Trim 1/4" from drawn line **(Fig. 2)** and press toward triangle **(Fig. 3)**. Place a 2 1/2" square on the opposite corner and repeat. Repeat on two remaining corners to make a **Square-in-a-Square Unit**. Make 20 Square-in-a-Square Units.

2. Sew a 2 1/2" x 4 1/2" Block A frame to each side of a Square-in-a-Square Unit. Press toward frames. Sew a 2 1/2" x 8 1/2" Block A frame to top and bottom of unit. Press toward frames to make **Block A**. Make 20 Block A's.

3. Sew a 2 1/2" x 4 1/2" Block B frame to each side of a 4 1/2" Block B center square **(Fig. 4)**. Press toward frames. Sew a 2 1/2" x 8 1/2" Block B frame to top and bottom of unit. Press toward frames to make **Block B**. Make 12 Block B's.

ASSEMBLING THE QUILT TOP

*Refer to **Quilt Top** for assembly.*

1. Arrange Blocks and setting triangles as shown in **Fig. 5**. Rotate Block B's to avoid seams lining up with Block A's.

2. Sew Blocks and large setting triangles into diagonal rows and press seam allowances in the opposite direction of the previous row. Sew small setting triangles to corners to complete **Quilt Top**. ***Note:*** *You will have [2] extra large setting triangles.*

COMPLETING THE QUILT

1. Follow **Quilting**, page 43, to mark, layer, and quilt as desired. Quilt shown is quilted with an allover meandering pattern.

2. Follow **Making a Hanging Sleeve**, page 45, if a hanging sleeve is desired.

3. Use **binding strips** and follow **Making Straight-Grain Binding**, page 45, to make binding. Follow **Attaching Binding with Mitered Corners**, page 46, to bind quilt.

CONNECT FOUR

For my alternate quilt, I simply changed the fabrics to bright solid colors and prints for a dramatic fun-loving quilt.

SHOPPING LIST

Yardage is based on 43"/44" wide fabric with a usable width of 40". Alternate colorway is given in parenthesis.

- ☐ 1 1/2 yds of white print (solid white) fabric for background
- ☐ 1/3 yd of red (teal) fabric for large squares
- ☐ 1/3 yd of green (yellow) fabric for large squares
- ☐ 1/4 yd of yellow (green) fabric for large square
- ☐ 1/4 yd ***each*** of 3 print fabrics for small squares
- ☐ 3 3/4 yds of fabric for backing
- ☐ 1/2 yd of fabric for binding

You will also need:

- ☐ 58" x 66" piece of batting

Finished Quilt Size: 50" x 58" (including border)

CUTTING THE PIECES

*Follow **Rotary Cutting**, page 39, to cut fabric. WOF = cut strips across width of fabric from selvage to selvage. Border is cut exact length. All measurements include 1/4" seam allowances.*

From fabric for background:

- Cut [1] 10 1/2" x WOF strip; from this strip, cut [3] 4 1/2" x 10 1/2" rectangles and [7] 2 1/2" x 10 1/2" rectangles.
- Cut [2] 8 1/2" x WOF strips.
  - From first strip, cut [1] 8 1/2" x 12 1/2" rectangle, [1] 8 1/2" x 8 1/2" square, [1] 6 1/2" x 8 1/2" rectangle, and [2] 2 1/2" x 8 1/2" rectangles.
  - From second strip, cut [3] 8 1/2" x 10 1/2" rectangles.
- Cut [2] 6 1/2" x WOF strips.
  - From first strip, cut [1] 6 1/2" x 12 1/2" rectangle, [1] 6 1/2" x 6 1/2" square, and [2] 4 1/2" x 6 1/2" rectangles.
  - From second strip, cut [13] 2 1/2" x 6 1/2" rectangles.
- Cut [1] 4 1/2" x WOF strip; from this strip, cut [1] 4 1/2" x 14 1/2" rectangle, [1] 4 1/2" x 12 1/2" rectangle, and [1] 4 1/2" x 4 1/2" square.
- Cut [1] 2 1/2" x WOF strip; from this strip, cut [1] 2 1/2" x 16 1/2" rectangle, [1] 2 1/2" x 12 1/2" rectangle, and [1] 2 1/2" x 4 1/2" rectangle.
- Cut [6] 4 1/2" x WOF border strips. ***Note:** The alternate colorway quilt does not have a border.*

From red fabric for large squares:

- Cut [4] 2 1/2" x WOF strips.
  - From first strip, cut [1] 2 1/2" x 22 1/2" rectangle and [1] 2 1/2" x 14 1/2" rectangle.
  - From second strip cut [1] 2 1/2" x 20 1/2" rectangle and [1] 2 1/2" x 10 1/2" rectangle.
  - From third strip, cut [3] 2 1/2" x 12 1/2" rectangles.
  - From fourth strip, cut [1] 2 1/2" x 14 1/2" rectangle, [1] 2 1/2" x 10 1/2" rectangle, and [1] 2 1/2" x 8 1/2" rectangle.

From green fabric for large squares:

- Cut [4] 2 1/2" x WOF strips.
  - From first strip, cut [1] 2 1/2" x 18 1/2" rectangle and [1] 2 1/2" x 16 1/2" rectangle.
  - From second strip, cut [2] 2 1/2" x 12 1/2" rectangles and [1] 2 1/2" x 6 1/2" rectangle.
  - From third strip, cut [4] 2 1/2" x 8 1/2" rectangles.
  - From fourth strip, cut [4] 2 1/2" x 4 1/2" rectangles.

From yellow fabric for large squares:

- Cut [3] 2 1/2" x WOF strips.
  - From first strip, cut [1] 2 1/2" x 16 1/2" rectangle and [1] 2 1/2" x 14 1/2" rectangle.
  - From second strip, cut [1] 2 1/2" x 12 1/2" rectangle, [1] 2 1/2" x 10 1/2" rectangle, [1] 2 1/2" x 4 1/2" rectangle, and [1] 2 1/2" x 2 1/2" square.
  - From third strip, cut [4] 2 1/2" x 6 1/2" rectangles.

From *each* of 3 fabrics for small squares:

- Cut [2] 6 1/2" x 6 1/2" squares.

From fabric for binding:

- Cut [6] 2 1/2" x WOF strips.

Sections

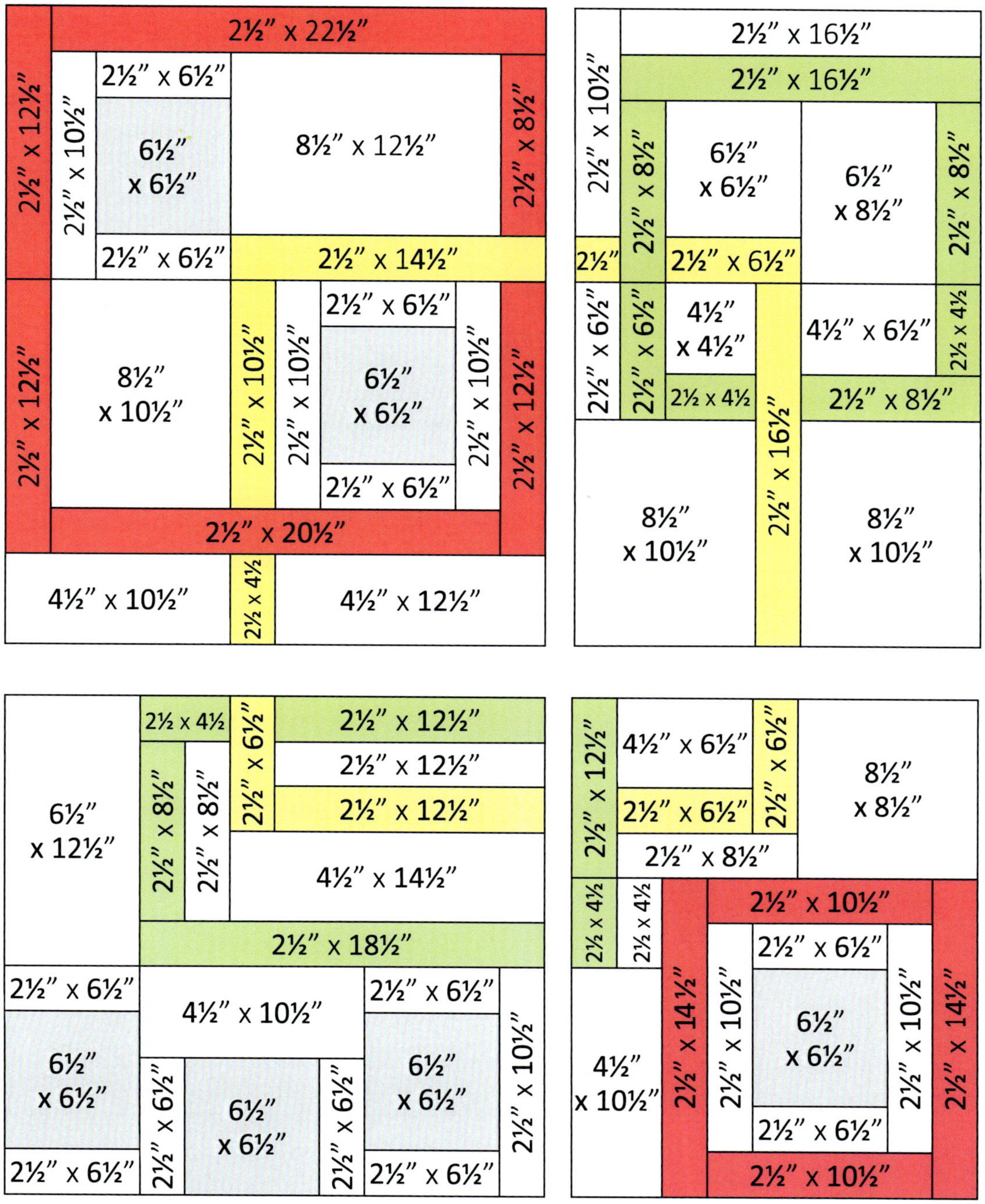
2½" x 22½"
2½" x 12½"
2½" x 10½"
2½" x 6½"
6½" x 6½"
8½" x 12½"
2½" x 8½"
2½" x 6½"
2½" x 14½"
2½" x 12½"
8½" x 10½"
2½" x 10½"
2½" x 10½"
2½" x 6½"
6½" x 6½"
2½" x 10½"
2½" x 12½"
2½" x 6½"
2½" x 20½"
4½" x 10½"
2½ x 4½
4½" x 12½"
2½" x 16½"
2½" x 16½"
2½" x 10½"
2½" x 8½"
6½" x 6½"
6½" x 8½"
2½" x 8½"
2½"
2½" x 6½"
2½" x 6½"
2½" x 6½"
4½" x 4½"
4½" x 6½"
2½ x 4½
2½ x 4½
2½" x 16½"
2½" x 8½"
8½" x 10½"
8½" x 10½"
6½" x 12½"
2½ x 4½
2½" x 8½"
2½" x 8½"
2½" x 6½"
2½" x 12½"
2½" x 12½"
2½" x 12½"
4½" x 14½"
2½" x 18½"
2½" x 6½"
4½" x 10½"
2½" x 6½"
6½" x 6½"
2½" x 6½"
6½" x 6½"
2½" x 6½"
6½" x 6½"
2½" x 10½"
2½" x 6½"
2½" x 6½"
2½" x 12½"
4½" x 6½"
2½" x 6½"
8½" x 8½"
2½" x 6½"
2½" x 8½"
2½ x 4½
2½ x 4½
2½" x 10½"
2½" x 6½"
4½" x 10½"
2½" x 14½"
2½" x 10½"
6½" x 6½"
2½" x 10½"
2½" x 14½"
2½" x 6½"
2½" x 10½"

ASSEMBLING THE QUILT TOP

*Follow **Machine Piecing** and **Pressing**, page 40, to make quilt top. Use 1/4" seam allowances throughout. Refer to **Quilt Top** for assembly.*

1. This quilt is pieced in sections. I recommend laying out the pieces on a design wall or flat surface before sewing. Sew each section together as shown. Press toward darker fabrics.

2. Sew these sections into two halves. Sew the two halves together to complete **Quilt Top Center**.

3. Trim selvages from [6] 4 1/2" x WOF border strips and sew together end to end. Cut [4] strips 50 1/2" long and sew a border to each side of quilt. Press toward border strips. Sew 50 1/2" border strips to top and bottom of quilt. Press toward border strips to complete **Quilt Top**.

COMPLETING THE QUILT

1. Follow **Quilting**, page 43, to mark, layer, and quilt as desired. Quilt shown is quilted with evenly spaced horizontal lines.

2. Follow **Making a Hanging Sleeve**, page 45, if a hanging sleeve is desired.

3. Use **binding strips** and follow **Making Straight-Grain Binding**, page 45, to make binding. Follow **Attaching Binding with Mitered Corners**, page 46, to bind quilt.

Quilt Top Center

Quilt Top

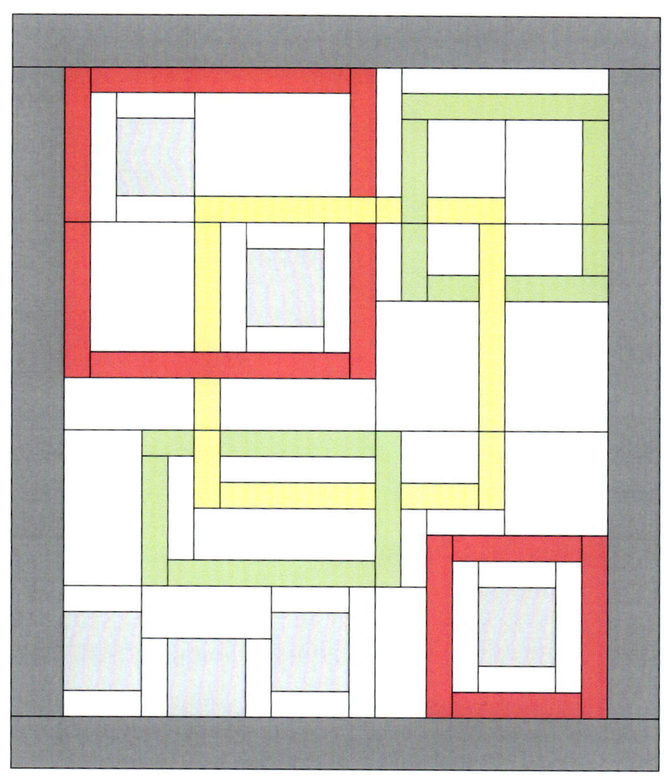

THE PLACES YOU'LL GO

Featuring the softest of printed flannels, this quilt will take him (or her) very far.

SHOPPING LIST

Yardage is based on 43"/44" wide fabric with a usable width of 40".

- ☐ 3/8 yd ***each*** of 5 print fabrics for backgrounds
- ☐ 1/2 yd of fabric for backgrounds of arrow points (blue solid)
- ☐ 1/2 yd of fabric for arrows (black print)
- ☐ 3/4 yd of fabric for border
- ☐ 3 5/8 yds of fabric for backing
- ☐ 1/2 yd of fabric for binding

You will also need:

- ☐ 56" x 64" piece of batting

Finished Quilt Size: 48" x 56"
Finished Block Size: 8" x 8"

CUTTING THE PIECES

*Follow **Rotary Cutting**, page 39, to cut fabric. WOF = cut strips across width of fabric from selvage to selvage. Border is cut exact length. All measurements include $^{1}/_{4}$" seam allowances.*

From *each* of 5 print fabrics for background:

- Cut [1] $8^{1}/_{2}$" x WOF strips; from this strip, cut [3] $8^{1}/_{2}$" squares.
- Cut [1] $3^{1}/_{2}$" x WOF strip; from this strip, cut [4] $3^{1}/_{2}$" x $8^{1}/_{2}$" rectangles.

From fabric for backgrounds of arrow points:

- Cut [1] $8^{1}/_{2}$" x WOF strip; from this strip, cut [1] $8^{1}/_{2}$" square.
  - Cut remainder of strip into [2] $3^{1}/_{2}$" strips and from these strips, cut [8] $3^{1}/_{2}$" x $4^{1}/_{2}$" rectangles.
- Cut [1] $4^{1}/_{2}$" x WOF strip; from this strip, cut [8] $4^{1}/_{2}$" squares.

From fabric for arrows:

- Cut [1] $8^{1}/_{2}$" x WOF strip; from this strip, cut [10] $2^{1}/_{2}$" x $8^{1}/_{2}$" rectangles and [4] $2^{1}/_{2}$" x $4^{1}/_{2}$" rectangles.
- Cut [1] $4^{1}/_{2}$" x WOF strip; from this strip, cut [4] $4^{1}/_{2}$" x $8^{1}/_{2}$" rectangles.

From fabric for border:

- Cut [5] $4^{1}/_{2}$" x WOF strips.

From fabric for binding:

- Cut [6] $2^{1}/_{2}$" x WOF strips.

MAKING THE UNITS

*Follow **Machine Piecing** and **Pressing**, page 40, to make quilt top. Use $^{1}/_{4}$" seam allowances throughout.*

1. Draw a diagonal line on the wrong side of [8] $4^{1}/_{2}$" arrow point background squares. With right sides together, place a $4^{1}/_{2}$" background square on the corner of $4^{1}/_{2}$" x $8^{1}/_{2}$" arrow fabric rectangle **(Fig. 1)**. Stitch diagonally on the drawn line **(Fig. 2)**. Trim $^{1}/_{4}$" from stitching line **(Fig. 3)** and press toward background fabric **(Fig. 4)**.

2. Add a second $4^{1}/_{2}$" arrow point background square to adjacent corner **(Fig. 5)**, trim $^{1}/_{4}$" from stitching line **(Fig. 6)** and press toward background fabric to complete **Flying Geese Unit**. Repeat to make a total of 4 Flying Geese Units.

3. Arrange [1] $2^{1}/_{2}$" x $4^{1}/_{2}$" arrow fabric rectangle and [2] $3^{1}/_{2}$" x $4^{1}/_{2}$" arrow background rectangles as shown. Sew a background rectangle to each side of arrow rectangle. Press toward background fabric to complete the **Background Unit**. Repeat to make a total of 4 background units.

4. Sew a flying geese unit to each background unit and press toward background unit to complete **Unit 1**. Repeat to make a total of 4 Unit 1's.

5. Sew a matching $3^{1}/_{2}$" x $8^{1}/_{2}$" background rectangle to each side of a $2^{1}/_{2}$" x $8^{1}/_{2}$" arrow rectangle to make **Unit 2**. Press toward darker fabric. Repeat to make a total of 10 Unit 2's.

ASSEMBLING THE QUILT TOP

*Refer to **Quilt Top** for assembly.*

1. Sew units and squares together in horizontal rows. Press seam allowances in opposite directions in each row. Sew rows together to complete **Quilt Top Center**.

2. Trim selvages from [5] $4^{1}/_{2}$" x WOF border strips and sew together end to end. Cut [4] border strips $48^{1}/_{2}$" long. Sew a border strip to each side of quilt. Press toward border strips. Sew a border strip to top and bottom of quilt. Press toward border strips to complete **Quilt Top**.

COMPLETING THE QUILT

1. Follow **Quilting**, page 43, to mark, layer, and quilt as desired. Quilt shown is quilted with randomly spaced vertical lines.

2. Follow **Making a Hanging Sleeve**, page 45, if a hanging sleeve is desired.

3. Use **binding strips** and follow **Making Straight-Grain Binding**, page 45, to make binding. Follow **Attaching Binding with Mitered Corners**, page 46, to bind quilt.

Fig. 1

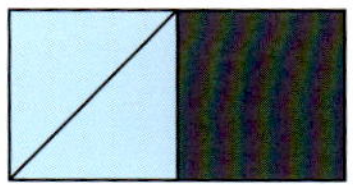

Fig. 2

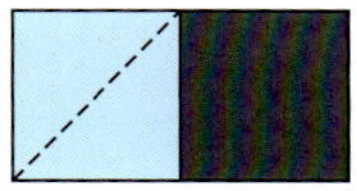

Fig. 3

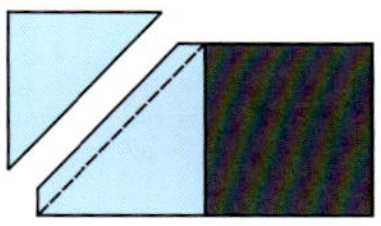

Fig. 4

Fig. 5

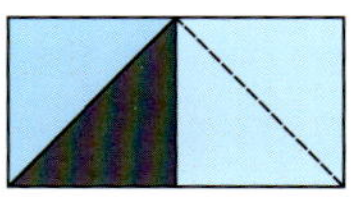

Fig. 6

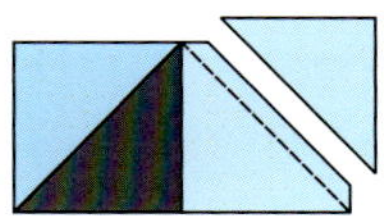

Flying Geese Unit (make 4)

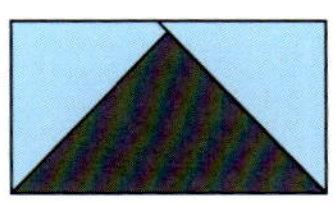

Background Unit (make 4)

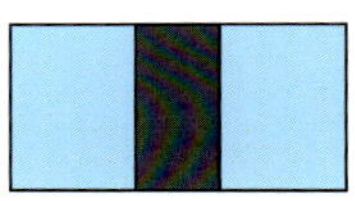

Unit 1 (make 4)

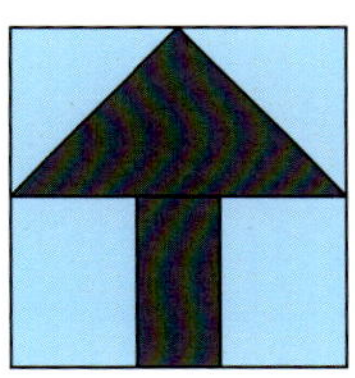

Unit 2
(make 10)

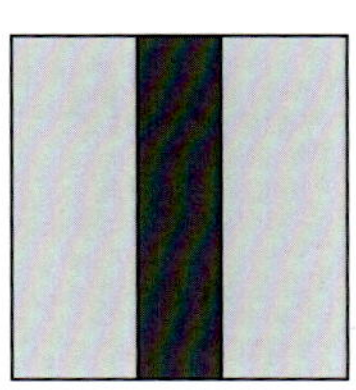

Quilt Top Center

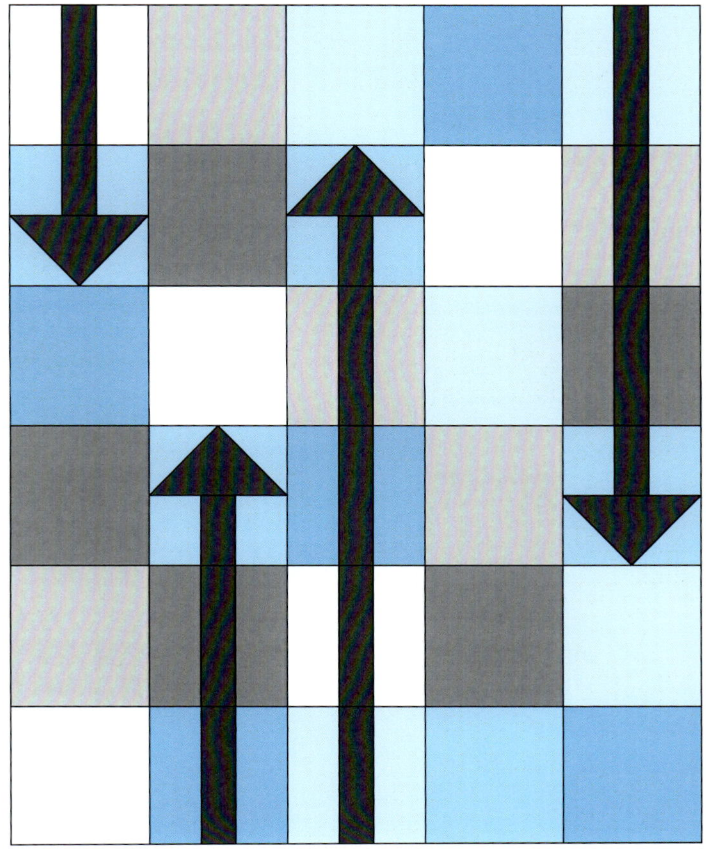

Quilt Top

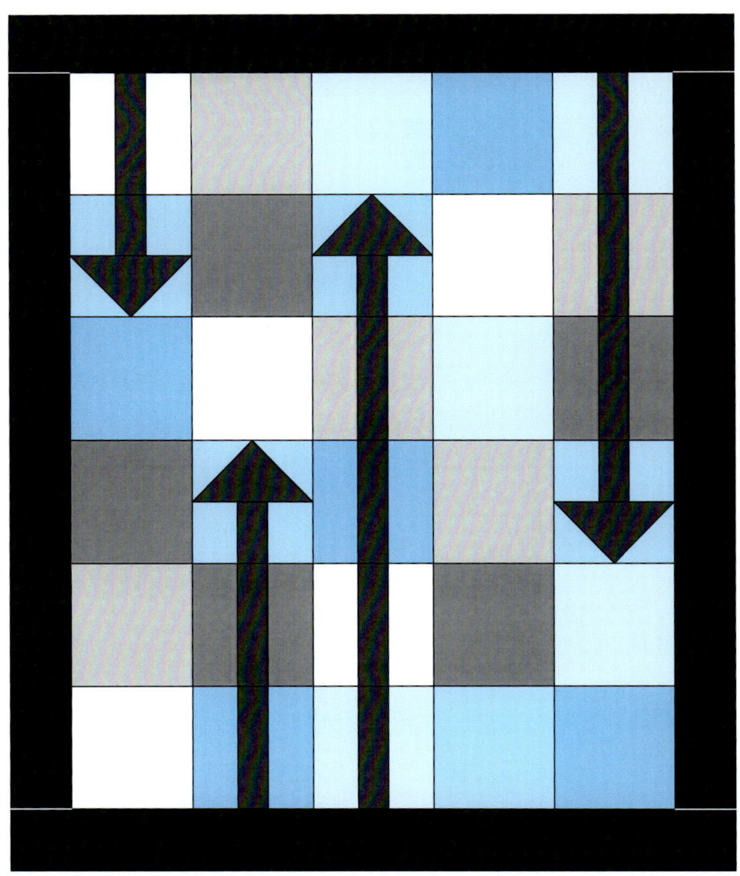

TIDDLY WINKS

This patterns appliquéd circles are a modern way to highlight fun, novelty prints.

SHOPPING LIST

Yardage is based on 43"/44" wide fabric with a usable width of 40".

- ☐ 3/4 yd of solid white fabric for background
- ☐ 3/4 yd of polka dot fabric for background
- ☐ 5/8 yd of print fabric for large circles
- ☐ 1/4 yd of print fabric for small circles
- ☐ 1/2 yd of fabric for inner border
- ☐ 7/8 yd of fabric for outer border
- ☐ 3 1/2 yds of fabric for backing
- ☐ 1/2 yd of fabric for binding

You will also need:

- ☐ 52" x 62" piece of batting
- ☐ 1 3/4 yds of 17" wide paper-backed fusible web
- ☐ Creative Grids™ Circle Savvy Ruler (optional)
- ☐ template plastic and permanent marker (optional)

Finished Quilt Size: 44" x 54"
Finished Block Size: 10" x 10"

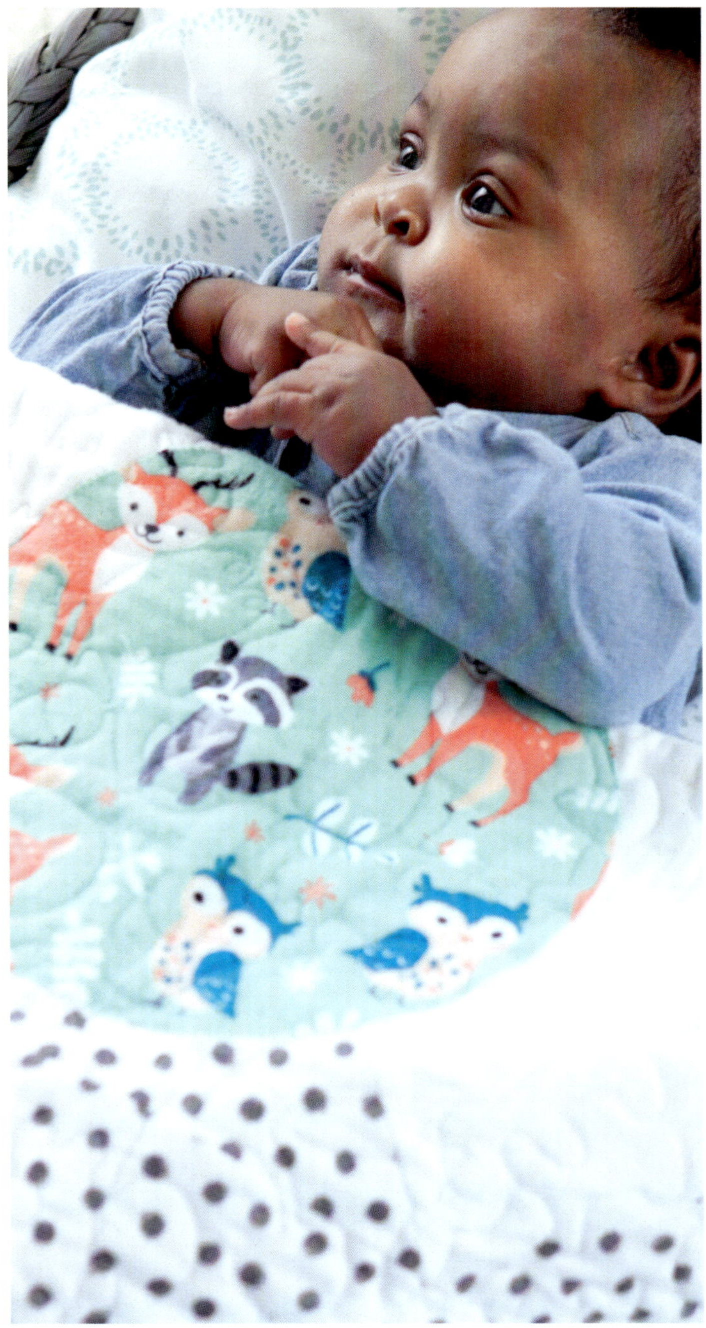

CUTTING THE PIECES

*Follow **Rotary Cutting**, page 39, to cut fabric. WOF = cut strips across width of fabric from selvage to selvage. Borders are cut exact length. All measurements include 1/4" seam allowances.*

From solid white background fabric:
- Cut [2] 11 1/4" x WOF strips; from these strips, cut [6] 11 1/4" squares. Cut each square twice diagonally.

From polka dot background fabric:
- Cut [2] 11 1/4" x WOF strips; from these strips, cut [6] 11 1/4" squares. Cut each square twice diagonally.

From print fabric for large circles:
- Cut [2] 9 1/2" x WOF strips; from these strips, cut [6] 9 1/2" squares.

From print fabric for small circles:
- Cut [1] 6 1/2" x WOF strip; from this strip, cut [6] 6 1/2" squares.

From inner border fabric:
- Cut [5] 2 1/2" x WOF strips.

From outer border fabric:
- Cut [5] 5 1/2" x WOF strips.

From binding fabric:
- Cut [6] 2 1/2" x WOF strips.

From fusible web:
- Cut [6] 9" squares and [6] 6" squares.

MAKING THE CIRCLE BLOCKS

*Follow **Machine Piecing** and **Pressing**, page 40, to make quilt top. Use 1/4" seam allowances throughout. I recommend the Creative Grids™ Circle Savvy Ruler for cutting perfect circles but you may use the patterns, page 31, instead.*

1. Arrange a solid white background triangle and a polka dot background triangle **(Fig. 1)**. Sew together along the short side and press toward the darker fabric. Repeat to make a total of [24] triangle pairs.

2. Sew two triangle pairs together **(Fig. 2)** and press to complete a **Background Block**. Block should measure 10 1/2" square, trim if necessary. Repeat to make a total of 12 background blocks.

3. Following fusible web manufacturer's instructions, fuse [1] 9" square of fusible web to the center of the wrong side of [1] 9 1/2" large circle square.

4. Fold the fused square into quarters and press. Align the FOLD LINES marked on the Circle Savvy Ruler with the folded edges of the fabric. Cut the arc using the 8 1/2" slot on the ruler to make a large circle **(Fig. 3)**. Repeat to make a total of 6 large circles.

5. Fuse [1] 6" square of fusible web to the center of the wrong side of [1] 6 1/2" small circle square.

Fig. 1 (make 24)

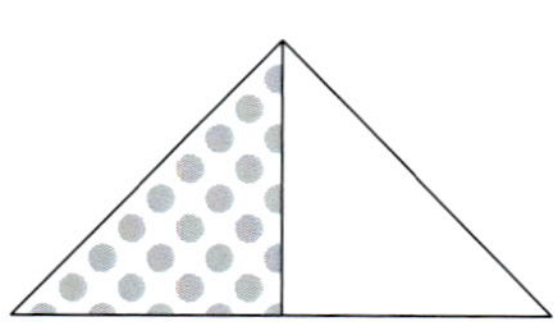

Fig. 2

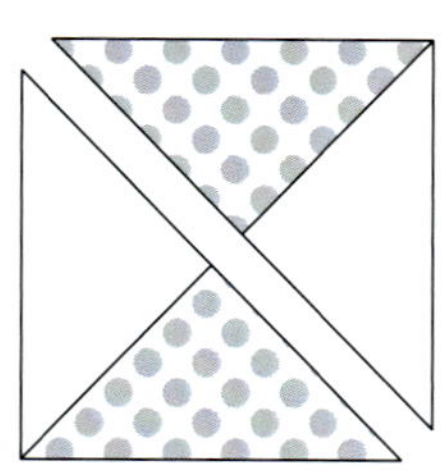

Background Block (make 12)

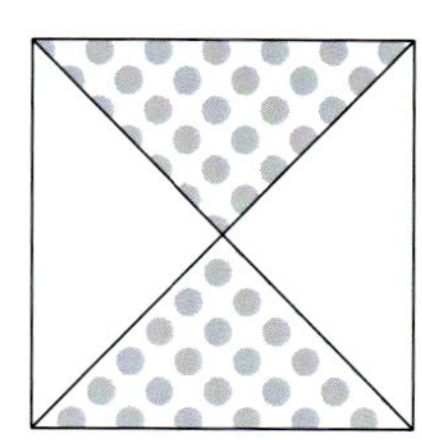

Fig. 3

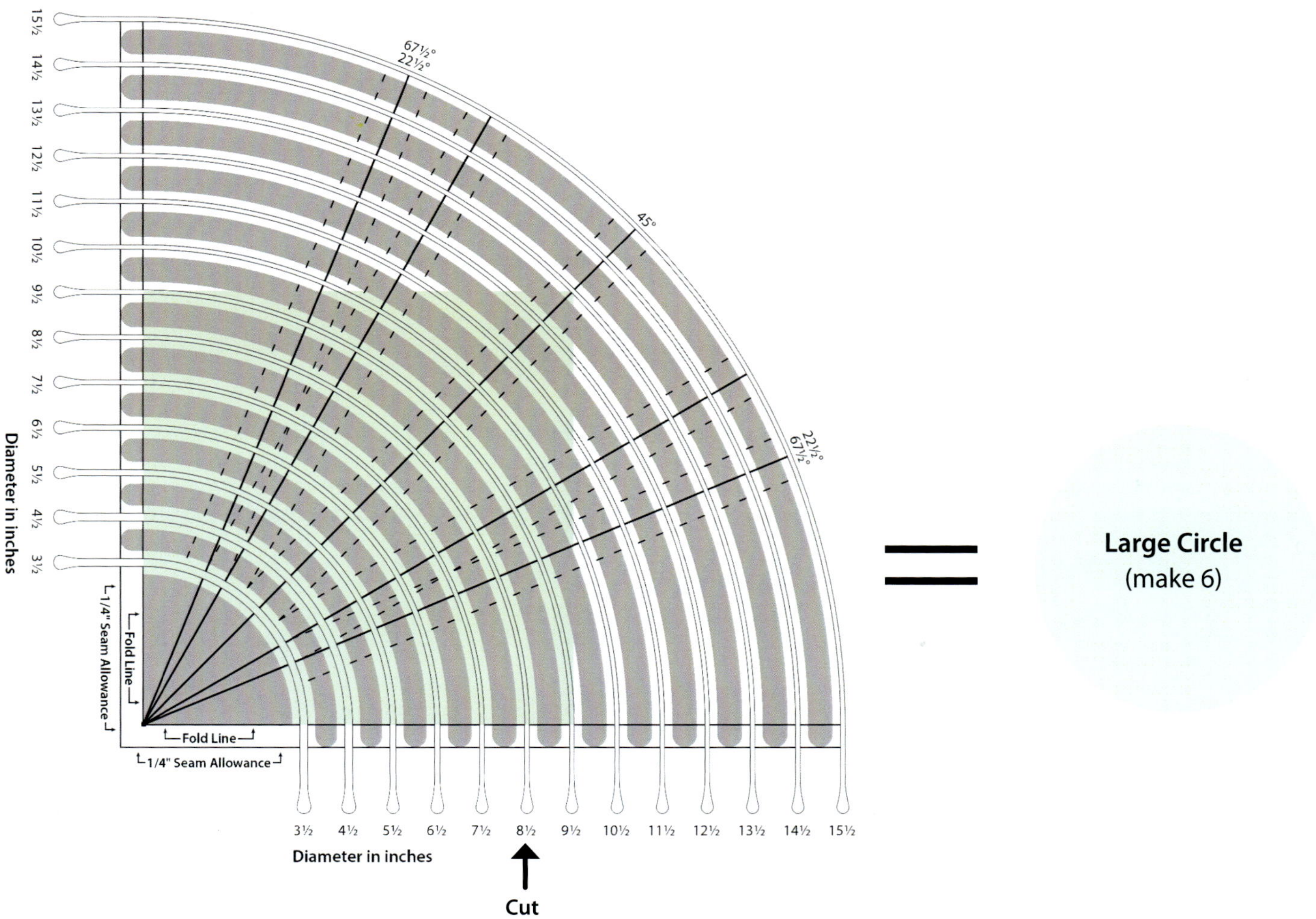

67½°
22½°
45°
22½°
67½°
15½
14½
13½
12½
11½
10½
9½
8½
7½
6½
5½
4½
3½
Diameter in inches
1/4" Seam Allowance
Fold Line
Fold Line
1/4" Seam Allowance
3½
4½
5½
6½
7½
8½
9½
10½
11½
12½
13½
14½
15½
Diameter in inches
Cut
Large Circle
(make 6)

6. Fold the fused square into quarters and press. Align the FOLD LINES marked on the Circle Savvy Ruler with the folded edges of the fabric. Cut the arc using the $5^1/_2$" slot on the ruler to make a small circle **(Fig. 4)**. Repeat to make a total of 6 small circles.

7. Following fusible web manufacturer's instructions, fuse [1] large circle to the center of a background block. Stitch around the circle using the appliqué stitch of your choice to make a **Circle Block**. I recommend Edge Stitch, Blanket Stitch, Zig Zag Stitch, or Satin Stitch. Repeat with remaining large and small circles for a total of 12 appliquéd blocks.

ASSEMBLING THE QUILT TOP

*Refer to **Quilt Top** for assembly.*

1. Arrange blocks as shown, alternating large and small circles. Sew blocks together into horizontal rows and press. Sew rows together and press to complete quilt top center.

2. Trim selvages from [5] $2^1/_2$" x WOF inner border strips and sew together end to end. Cut [2] strips $40^1/_2$" long and sew a border strip to each side of quilt. Press toward border strips. Cut [2] strips $34^1/_2$" long and sew to top and bottom of quilt. Press toward border strips.

Fig. 4

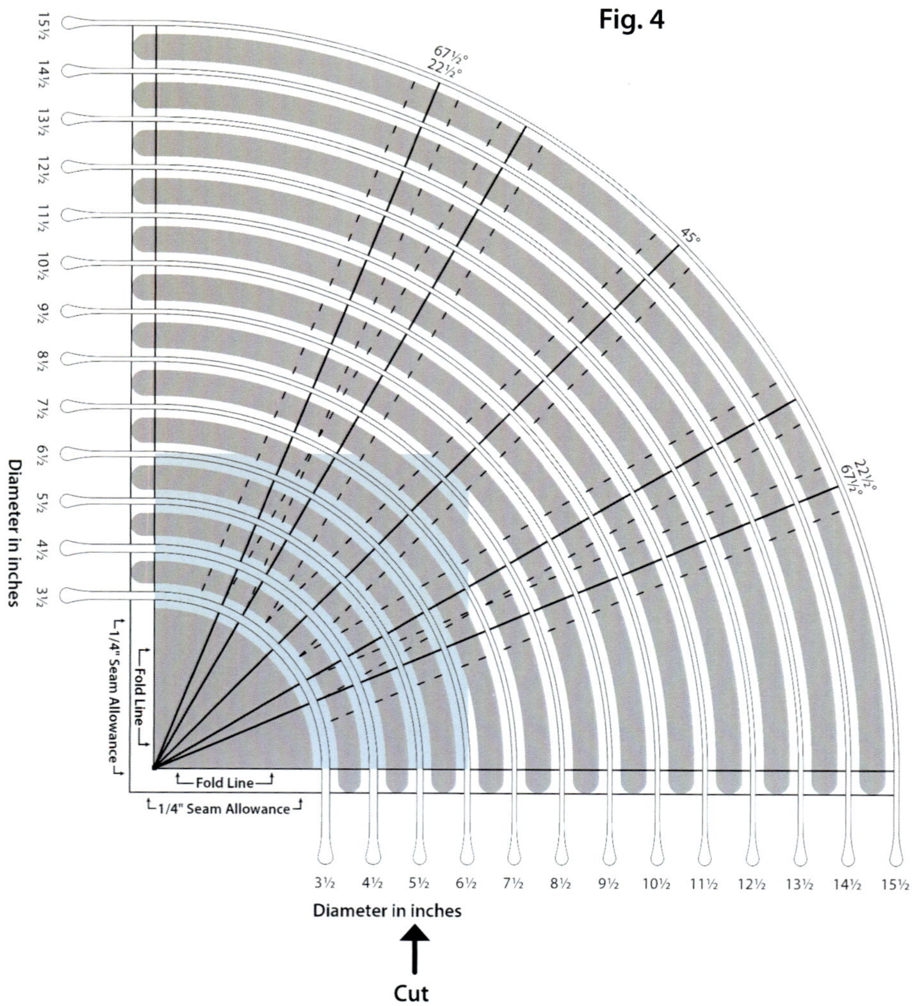

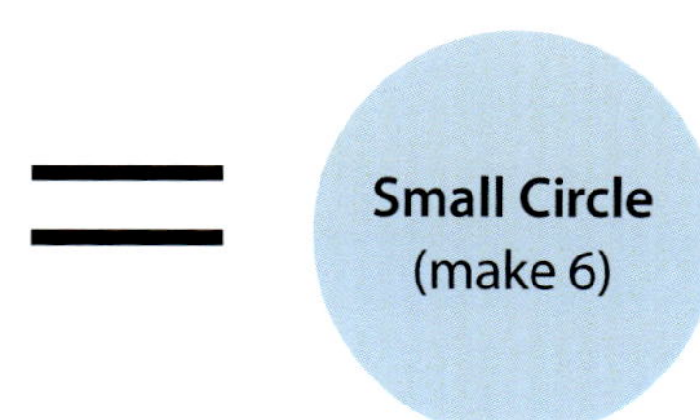

Note: For **Fig. 3**, white fabric is shown in blue for clarity.

Circle Block (make 12 total)

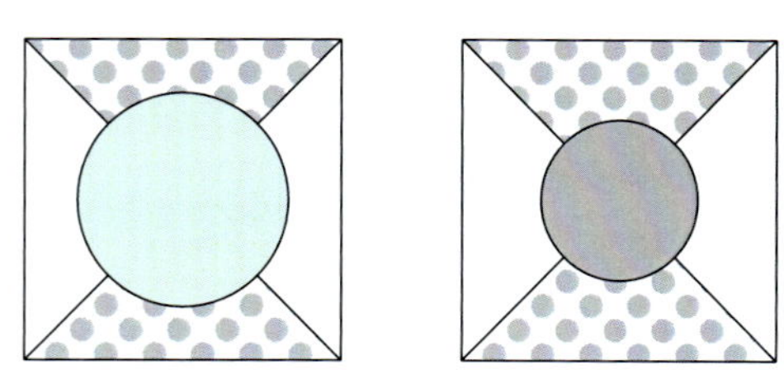

3. Trim selvages from [5] 5½" x WOF outer border strips and sew together end to end. Cut [4] strips 44½" long. Sew a border strip to each side of quilt. Press toward border strips. Sew a border strip to top and bottom of quilt. Press toward border strips to complete **Quilt Top**.

Quilt Top

COMPLETING THE QUILT

1. Follow **Quilting**, page 43, to mark, layer, and quilt as desired. Quilt shown is quilted with an all-over pattern of swirls and animals.

2. Follow **Making a Hanging Sleeve**, page 45, if a hanging sleeve is desired.

3. Use **binding strips** and follow **Making Straight-Grain Binding**, page 45, to make binding. Follow **Attaching Binding with Mitered Corners**, page 46, to bind quilt.

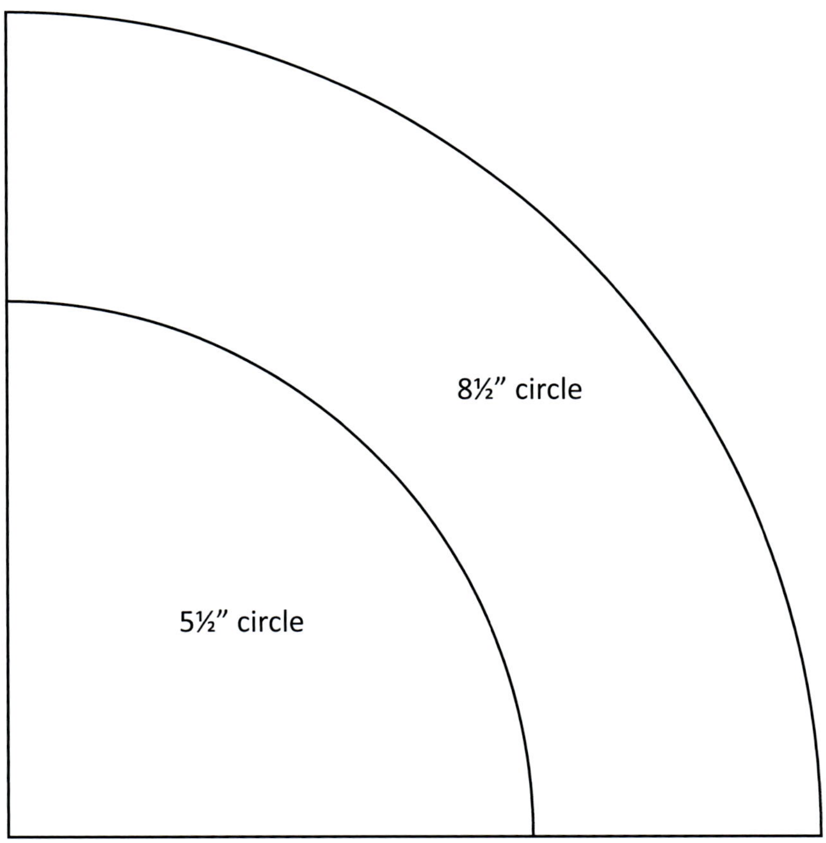

Circle

Option for Cutting Circles:
Lay the template plastic on the pattern and trace along the 8½" template lines. Reposition template plastic and repeat for 5½" template lines. Cut templates from plastic. Fold the fused square in quarters and press. Align the straight edges of each template with the bottom and left folded edges of a fused square. Cut along curved edge of template.

WHIRLIGIG

Use a rainbow of solid colors or prints to create this graphic quilt.

SHOPPING LIST

Yardage is based on 43"/44" wide fabric with a usable width of 40".

- ☐ 2 1/4 yds of solid white fabric for background
- ☐ 1/4 yd **each** of 15 solid color fabrics
- ☐ 3 1/8 yds of fabric for backing
- ☐ 1/2 yd of fabric for binding

You will also need:

- ☐ 2 5/8 yds of 17" wide paper-backed fusible web
- ☐ 56" x 56" piece of batting
- ☐ Creative Grids™ Circle Savvy Ruler (optional)
- ☐ template plastic and permanent marker (optional)

Finished Quilt Size: 48" x 48"

CUTTING THE PIECES

Before cutting, arrange your fabrics in order by color to determine which fabrics will be at the top and bottom of the quilt. The six top/bottom fabrics are cut differently than the nine center fabrics. Follow ***Rotary Cutting****, page 39, to cut fabric. WOF = cut strips across width of fabric from selvage to selvage. All measurements include 1/4" seam allowances.*

From solid white background fabric:

- Cut [5] 8 1/2" x WOF strips; from these strips, cut [34] 4 1/2" x 8 1/2" rectangles.
- Cut [4] 5" x WOF strips; from these strips, cut [30] 5" squares.
- Cut [2] 4 1/2" x WOF strips; from these strips, cut [16] 4 1/2" squares.

From each of 6 top/bottom solid colors:

- Cut [1] 5" x WOF strip; from this strip, cut [2] 5" squares. Trim remainder of strip to 4 1/2" wide and cut [3] 4 1/2" x 8 1/2" rectangles.

From each of 9 center solid colors:

- Cut [1] 5" x WOF strip; from this strip, cut [2] 5" squares. Trim remainder of strip to 4 1/2" wide and cut [2] 4 1/2" x 8 1/2" rectangles.

From paper-backed fusible web:

- Cut [19] 4 1/2" x WOF strips; from these strips, cut [30] 4 1/2" x 8 1/2" rectangles and [12] 4 1/2" squares.

From fabric for binding:

- Cut [6] 2 1/2" x WOF strips.

MAKING THE BLOCKS

Follow ***Machine Piecing*** *and* ***Pressing****, page 40, to make quilt top. Use 1/4" seam allowances throughout. I recommend the Creative Grids™ Circle Savvy Ruler for cutting perfect quarter- and half-circles but you may use the patterns, page 38, instead.*

1. Draw a diagonal line on the wrong side of [30] 5" white background squares. With right sides together, place a 5" background square on top of a 5" solid color square. Stitch ¼" on each side of drawn line **(Fig. 1)**. Cut along drawn line **(Fig. 2)** and press toward darker fabric to make 2 **half-square triangles**. Trim half-square triangle to 4 1/2" square. Repeat with remaining 5" squares to yield a total of [60] half-square triangle units.

2. Arrange four matching half-square triangle together. Sew units into pairs and press. Sew pairs together to complete **Block**. Repeat to make a total of 15 blocks.

3. Set aside four 4 1/2" white background squares for corner squares. Following fusible web manufacturer's instructions, center and fuse [1] 4 1/2" square of fusible web to the wrong side of each remaining 4 1/2" white background square.

Fig. 1

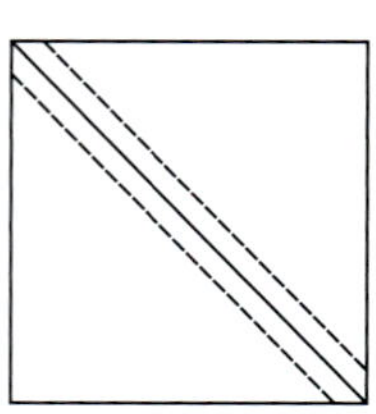

Fig. 2

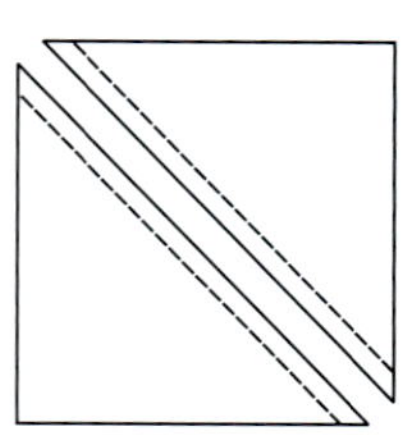

Half-Square Triangle
(make 60)

Block
(make 15)

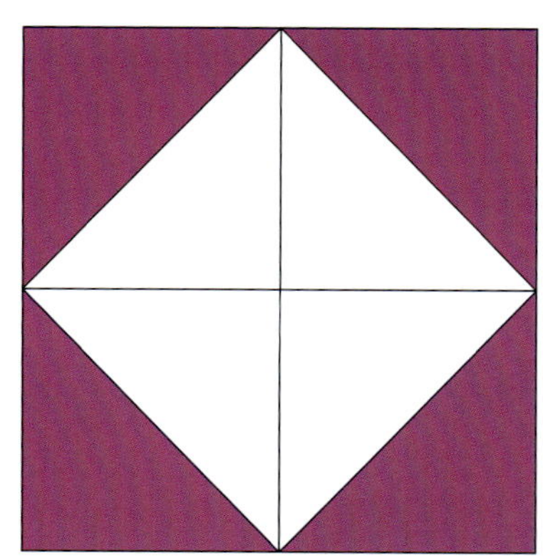

4. Align the SEAM ALLOWANCE lines marked on the Creative Grids™ Circle Savvy Ruler with the bottom and left edges of the fabric. Cut the arc using the 8" slot on the ruler **(Fig. 3)** to make a background quarter circle. Repeat to make a total of 12 background quarter circles.

5. Following fusible web manufacturer's instructions, center and fuse [1] $4^1/_2$" x $8^1/_2$" rectangle of fusible web to the wrong side of [1] $4^1/_2$" x $8^1/_2$" solid color rectangle. Repeat to apply fusible web to all $4^1/_2$" x $8^1/_2$" solid color rectangles.

Fig. 3

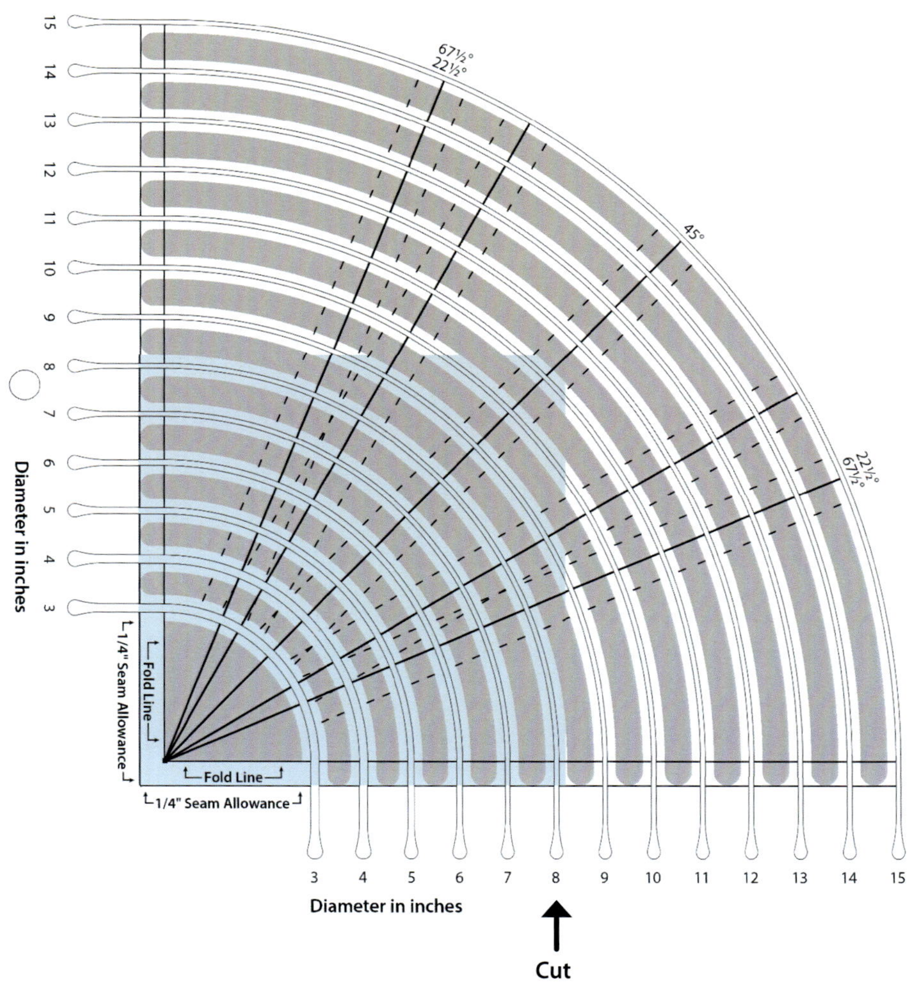

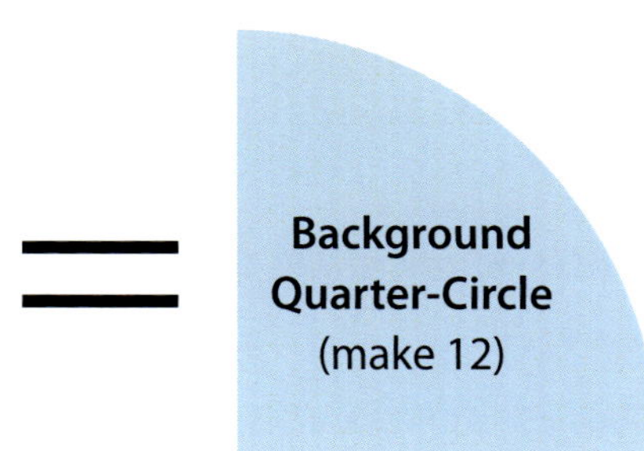

Note: For **Fig. 3**, white fabric is shown in blue for clarity.

6. Fold the fused rectangle in half lengthwise and press. Align the FOLD LINE marked on the Creative Grids™ Circle Savvy Ruler with the folded edges of the fabric and the bottom SEAM ALLOWANCE line with the bottom raw edge of fabric. Cut the arc using the 8" slot on the ruler to make a half circle **(Fig. 4)**. Repeat to make a total of 30 half circles.

7. Following fusible web manufacturer's instructions, fuse [1] background quarter-circle to each end of a $4^{1}/_{2}$" x $8^{1}/_{2}$" top/bottom solid color rectangle, aligning the bottom edges to make a **Quarter-Circle Block**. Stitch around the arc using the appliqué stitch of your choice. I recommend Edge Stitch, Blanket Stitch, Zig Zag Stitch, or Satin Stitch. Repeat with remaining quarter circles and 5 top/bottom rectangles to yield 1 quarter-circle block of each top/bottom fabric.

8. Following fusible web manufacturer's instructions, fuse [1] solid color half-circle to the bottom edge of a $4^{1}/_{2}$" x $8^{1}/_{2}$" background rectangle. Stitch around the arc using the appliqué stitch of your choice to make a **Half-Circle Block**. Repeat with remaining half-circles and $4^{1}/_{2}$" x $8^{1}/_{2}$" background rectangles for a total of 30 Half-Circle Blocks.

Fig. 4

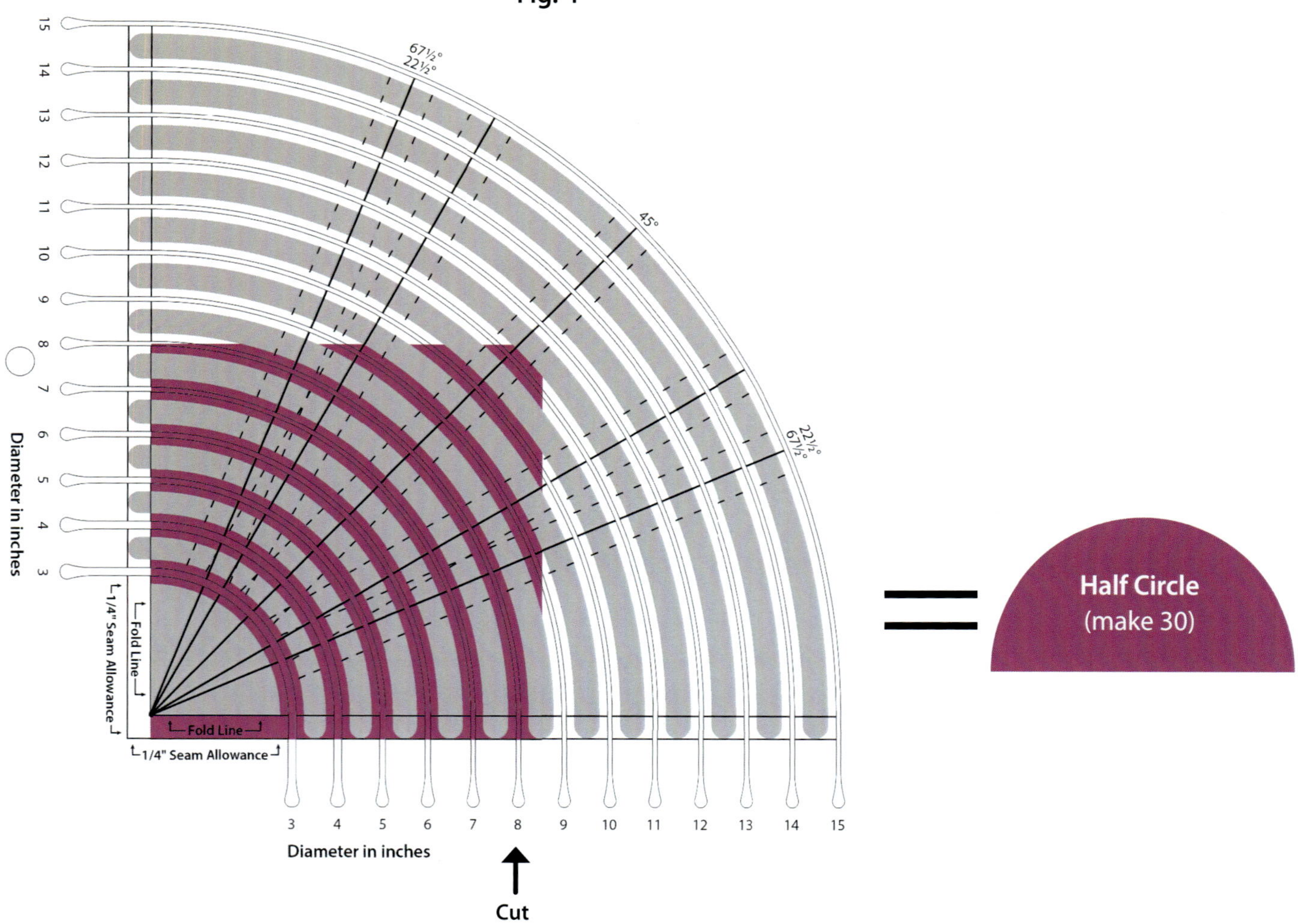

ASSEMBLING THE QUILT TOP

1. Arrange all units as shown. Sew blocks together into horizontal rows and press. Sew rows together and press to complete Quilt Top.

COMPLETING THE QUILT

1. Follow **Quilting**, page 43, to mark, layer, and quilt as desired. Quilt shown is quilted with diamonds and circles in the white center of each whirligig, an allover swirl pattern in each whirligig, and vertical lines in each white top and bottom border.
2. Follow **Making a Hanging Sleeve**, page 45, if a hanging sleeve is desired.
3. Use **binding strips** and follow **Making Straight-Grain Binding**, page 45, to make binding. Follow **Attaching Binding with Mitered Corners**, page 46, to bind quilt.

Quarter-Circle Block (make 6)

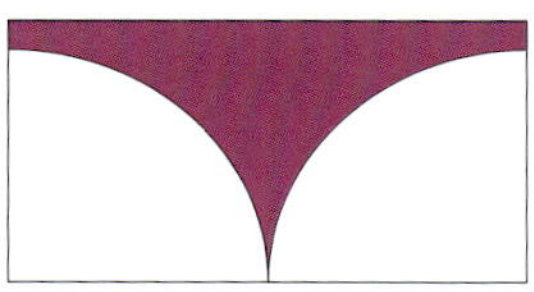

Half-Circle Block (make 30)

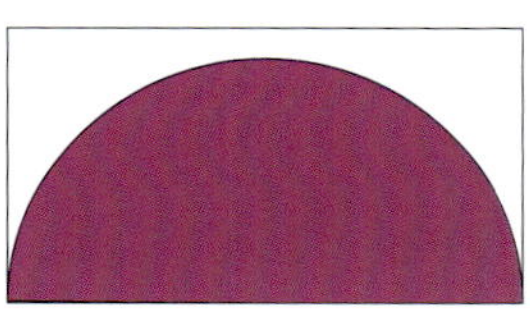

Quilt Top Diagram

Option for Cutting Quarter-Circles and Half-Circles: For quarter-circles, lay the template plastic on the quarter-circle pattern and trace. Cut template from plastic. Align the straight edges of the quarter-circle template with the bottom and left edges of the fused square. Cut along curved edge of template.

For half-circles, lay the template plastic on the half-circle pattern and trace. Cut template from plastic. Fold the fused rectangle in half and press. Align the left straight edge of the template with the folded edge, and the bottom straight edge of the template with the bottom edge of the fused rectangles. Cut along curved edge of template.

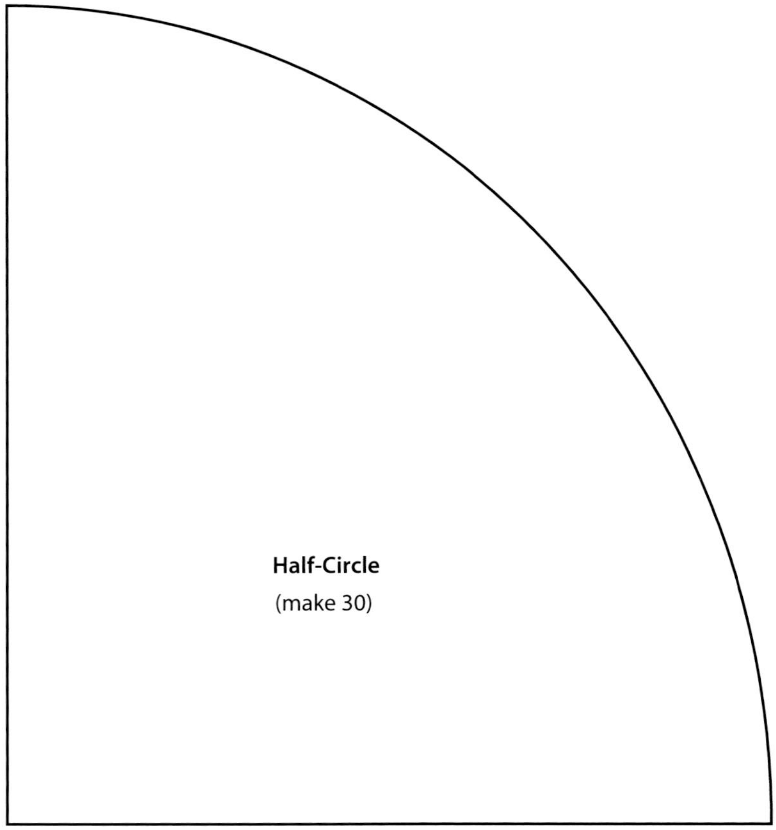

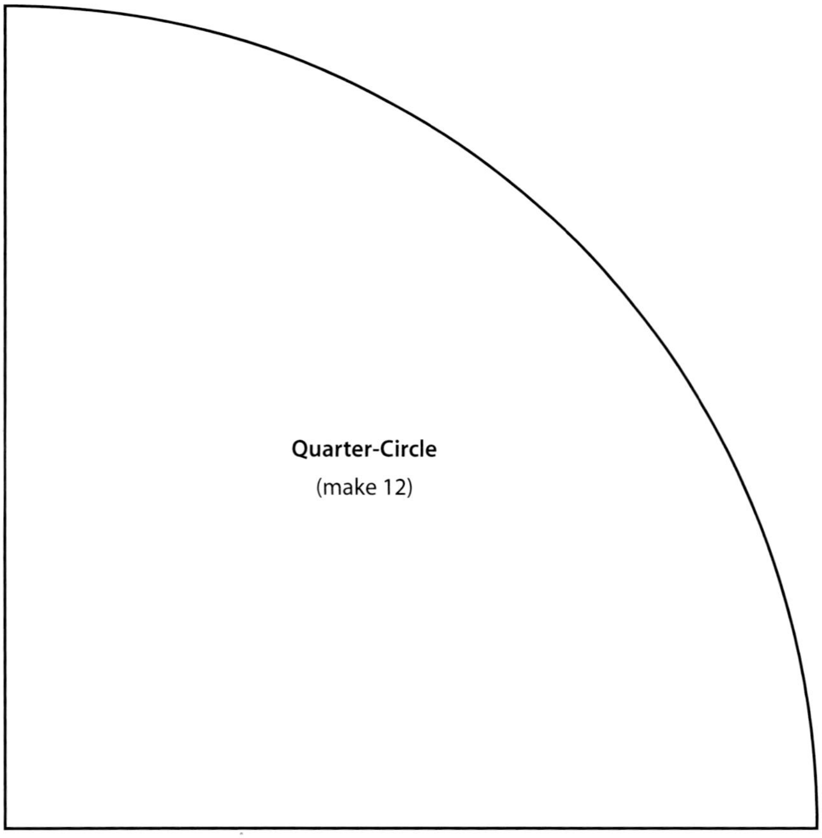

General Instructions

To make your quilting easier and more enjoyable, we encourage you to carefully read all of the general instructions, study the color photographs, and familiarize yourself with the individual project instructions before beginning a project.

FABRICS

SELECTING FABRICS

Choose high-quality, medium-weight 100% cotton fabrics. All-cotton fabrics hold a crease better, fray less, and are easier to quilt than cotton/polyester blends.

Yardage requirements listed for each project are based on 43"/44" wide fabric with a "usable" width of 40" after shrinkage and trimming selvages. Actual usable width will probably vary slightly from fabric to fabric. Our recommended yardage lengths should be adequate for occasional re-squaring of fabric when many cuts are required.

PREPARING FABRICS

We recommend that all fabrics be washed, dried, and pressed before cutting. If fabrics are not pre-washed, washing the finished quilt will cause shrinkage and give it a more "antiqued" look and feel. Bright and dark colors, which may run, should always be washed before cutting. After washing and drying fabric, fold lengthwise with wrong sides together and matching selvages.

ROTARY CUTTING

- Place fabric on work surface with fold closest to you.
- Cut all strips from the selvage-to-selvage width of the fabric unless otherwise indicated in project instructions.
- Square left edge of fabric using rotary cutter and rulers **(Figs. 1-2)**.
- To cut each strip required for a project, place ruler over cut edge of fabric, aligning desired marking on ruler with cut edge; make cut **(Fig. 3)**.
- When cutting several strips from a single piece of fabric, it is important to make sure that cuts remain at a perfect right angle to the fold; square fabric as needed.

Fig. 1

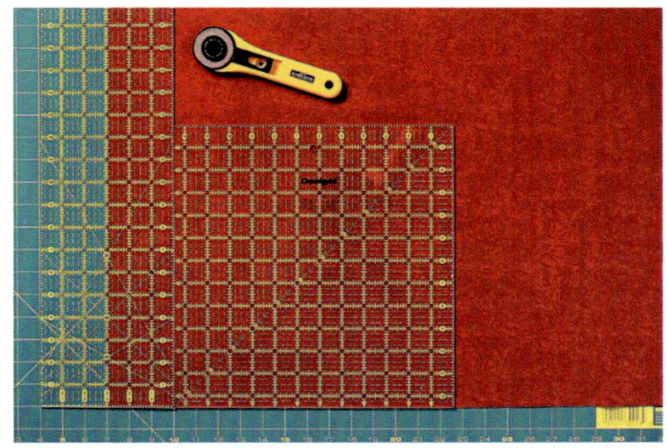

Fig. 2

Fig. 3

MACHINE PIECING

Precise cutting, followed by accurate piecing, will ensure that all pieces of quilt top fit together well.

- Set sewing machine stitch length for approximately 11 stitches per inch.
- Use neutral-colored general-purpose sewing thread (not quilting thread) in needle and in bobbin.
- An accurate 1/4" seam allowance is *essential*. Presser feet that are 1/4" wide are available for most sewing machines.
- When piecing, always place pieces right sides together and match raw edges; pin if necessary.
- Chain piecing saves time and will usually result in more accurate piecing.
- Trim away points of seam allowances that extend beyond edges of sewn pieces.

SEWING ACROSS SEAM INTERSECTIONS

When sewing across intersection of two seams, place pieces right sides together and match seams exactly, making sure seam allowances are pressed in opposite directions **(Fig. 4)**.

Fig. 4

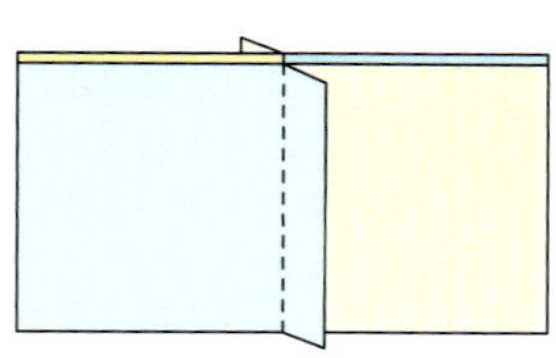

SEWING SHARP POINTS

To ensure sharp points when joining triangular or diagonal pieces, stitch across the center of the "X" (shown in pink) formed on wrong side by previous seams **(Fig. 5)**.

Fig. 5

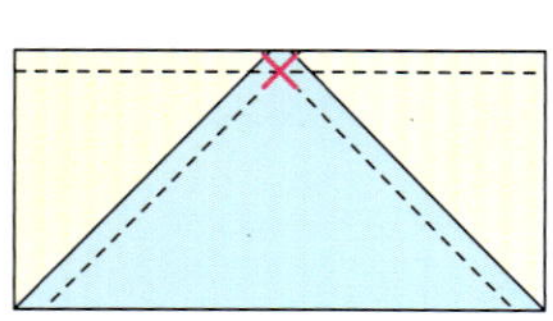

PRESSING

- Use steam iron set on "Cotton" for all pressing.
- Press after sewing each seam.
- Seam allowances are almost always pressed to one side, usually toward darker fabric. However, to reduce bulk it may occasionally be necessary to press seam allowances toward the lighter fabric or even to press them open.
- To prevent dark fabric seam allowance from showing through light fabric, trim darker seam allowance slightly narrower than lighter seam allowance.
- To press long seams, such as those in long strip sets, without curving or other distortion, lay strips across width of the ironing board.
- When sewing blocks into rows, seam allowances may be pressed in one direction in odd numbered rows and in the opposite direction in even numbered rows. When sewing rows together, press seam allowances in one direction.

MACHINE APPLIQUÉ

PREPARING FUSIBLE APPLIQUÉS

White or light-colored fabrics may need to be lined with fusible interfacing before applying fusible web to prevent darker fabrics from showing through.

1. Place paper-backed fusible web, paper side up, over appliqué pattern. Trace pattern onto paper side of web with pencil as many times as indicated in project instructions for a single fabric.
2. Follow manufacturer's instructions to fuse traced patterns to wrong side of fabrics. Do not remove paper backing.
3. Cut out appliqué pieces along traced lines. Remove paper backing from all pieces.

APPLIQUÉ

Appliqués may be finished with a Blanket Stitch, Satin Stitch, Zigzag Stitch, or Edge Stitch. An Edge Stitch is done by merely straight stitching near the raw edge of the appliqué. The following methods may also be used.

Blanket Stitch Appliqué

Many sewing machines feature a Blanket Stitch. Refer to your owner's manual for machine set-up. If your machine does not have this stitch, try some of the decorative stitches on your machine until you are satisfied with the look of your appliqué.

1. Pin stabilizer, such as paper or any of the commercially available products, on wrong side of background fabric before stitching appliqués in place.
2. Thread sewing machine with general-purpose thread; use general-purpose thread that matches background in bobbin.
3. Set sewing machine for a medium (approximately 1/8") stitch width and a short stitch length. Slightly loosening the top tension may yield a smoother stitch.
4. Begin by stitching two or three stitches in place (drop feed dogs or set stitch length at 0) to anchor thread. Most of the Blanket Stitch should be on the appliqué with the right edge of the stitch falling at the outside edge of the appliqué. Stitch over all exposed raw edges of appliqué pieces.
5. *(**Note:** Dots on **Figs. 6-12** indicate where to leave needle in fabric when pivoting.)* For outside corners, stitch just past corner, stopping with needle in background fabric **(Fig. 6)**. Raise presser foot. Pivot project, lower presser foot, and take an angled stitch. Raise presser foot. Pivot project, lower presser foot and stitch adjacent side **(Fig. 7)**.

Fig. 6

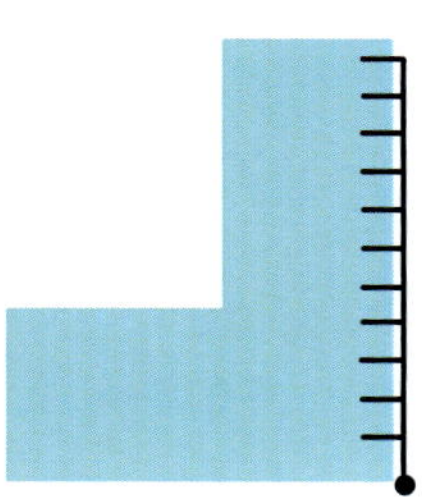

Fig. 7

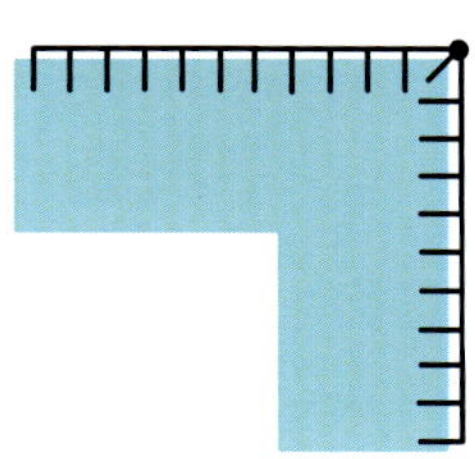

6. For inside corners, stitch to the corner, stopping with needle in background fabric **(Fig. 8)**. Raise presser foot. Pivot project, lower presser foot, and take an angled stitch. Raise presser foot. Pivot project, lower presser foot and stitch adjacent side **(Fig. 9)**.

Fig. 8

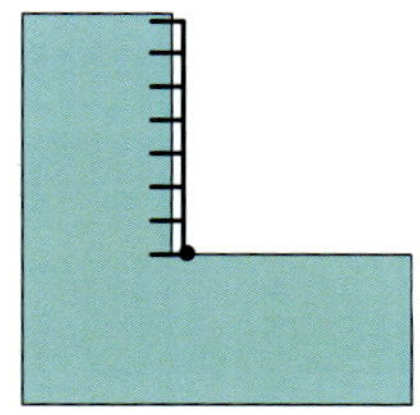

Fig. 9

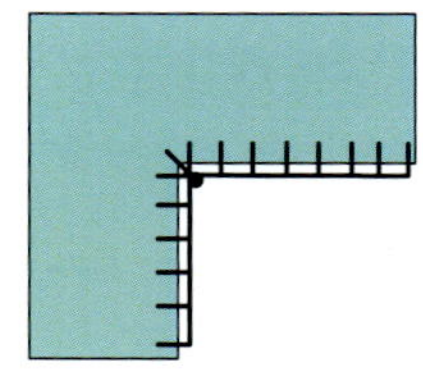

7. When stitching outside curves, stop with needle in background fabric. Raise presser foot and pivot project as needed. Lower presser foot and continue stitching, pivoting as often as necessary to follow curve **(Fig. 10)**.

Fig. 10

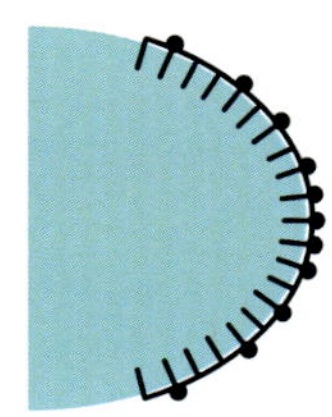

8. When stitching inside curves, stop with needle in background fabric. Raise presser foot and pivot project as needed. Lower presser foot and continue stitching, pivoting as often as necessary to follow curve **(Fig. 11)**.

Fig. 11

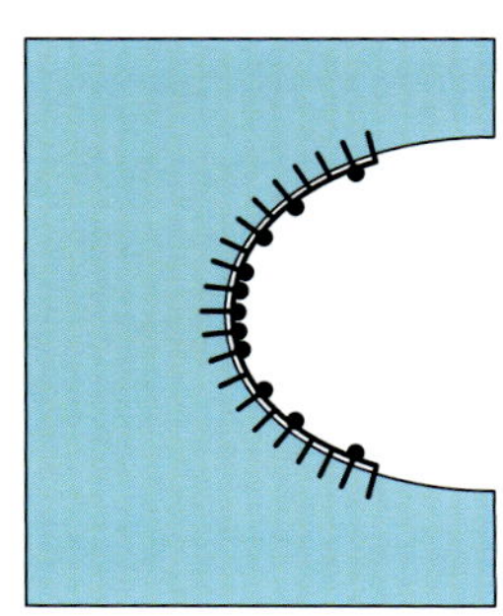

9. When stitching outside points, stop one stitch short of the point. Raise presser foot. Pivot project slightly, lower presser foot and make one angled Stitch 1. Take the next stitch, stop at point and pivot so that Stitch 2 will be perpendicular to the point. Pivot slightly to make Stitch 3. Continue stitching around appliqué **(Fig. 12)**.

Fig. 12

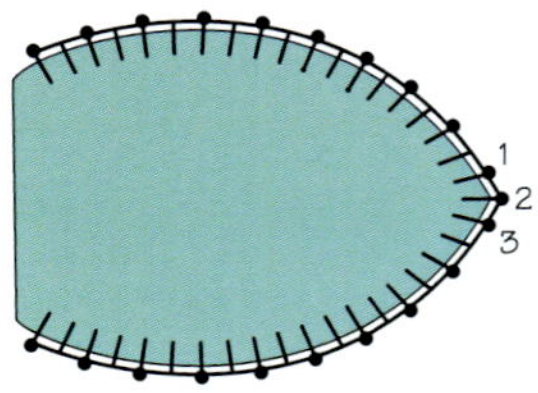

10. End by stitching two or three stitches in place (drop feed dogs or set stitch length at 0) to anchor thread.
11. Carefully tear away stabilizer.

Satin Stitch and Zig Zag Appliqué

A good satin stitch is a thick, smooth, almost solid line of zigzag stitching that covers the exposed raw edges of appliqué pieces. Zig Zag Appliqué is done in the same manner using a longer stitch length.

1. Pin stabilizer, such as paper or any of the commercially available products, on wrong side of background fabric before stitching appliqués in place.
2. Thread sewing machine with general-purpose thread; use general-purpose thread that matches background fabric in bobbin.
3. Set sewing machine for a medium (approximately 1/8") zigzag stitch and a short stitch length. Slightly loosening the top tension may yield a smoother stitch.
4. Begin by stitching two or three stitches in place (drop feed dogs or set stitch length at 0) to anchor thread. Most of the Satin Stitch should be on the appliqué with the right edge of the stitch falling at the outside edge of the appliqué. Stitch over all exposed raw edges of appliqué pieces.
5. (***Note:*** Dots on ***Figs. 13-18*** indicate where to leave needle in fabric when pivoting.) For outside corners, stitch just past corner, stopping with needle in background fabric **(Fig. 13)**. Raise presser foot. Pivot project, lower presser foot, and stitch adjacent side **(Fig. 14)**.

Fig.13

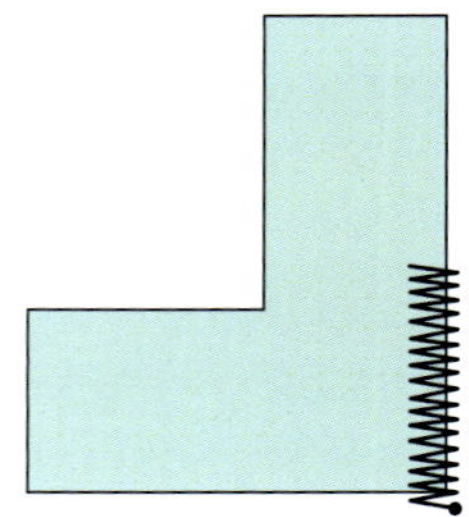

Fig.14

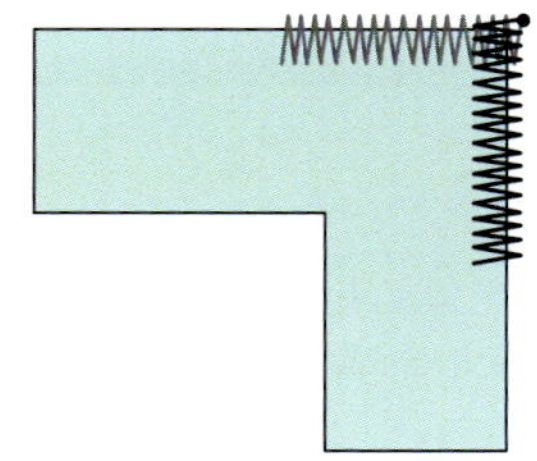

6. For inside corners, stitch just past corner, stopping with needle in appliqué fabric **(Fig. 15)**. Raise presser foot. Pivot project, lower presser foot, and stitch adjacent side **(Fig. 16)**.

Fig.15

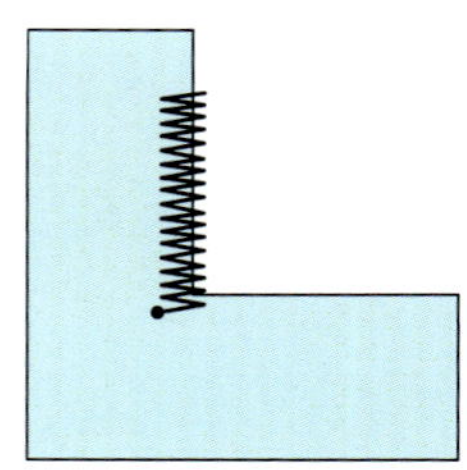

Fig.16

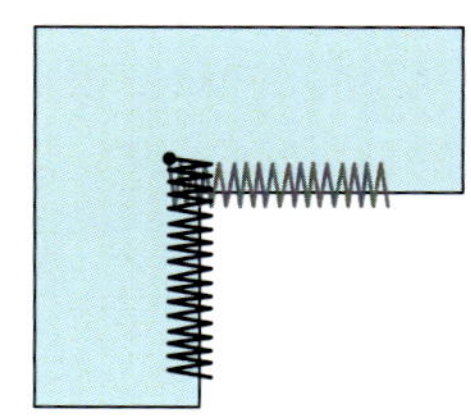

7. When stitching outside curves, stop with needle in background fabric. Raise presser foot and pivot project as needed. Lower presser foot and continue stitching, pivoting as often as necessary to follow curve **(Fig. 17)**.

Fig. 17

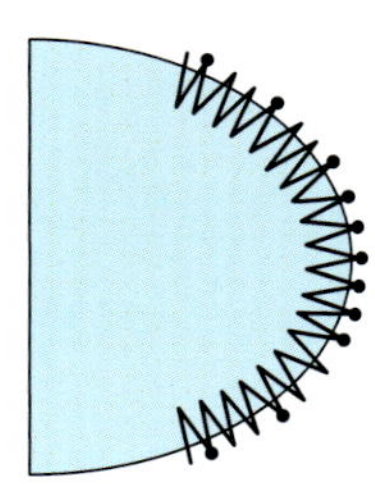

8. When stitching inside curves, stop with needle in appliqué fabric. Raise presser foot and pivot project as needed. Lower presser foot and continue stitching, pivoting as often as necessary to follow curve **(Fig. 18)**.

Fig. 18

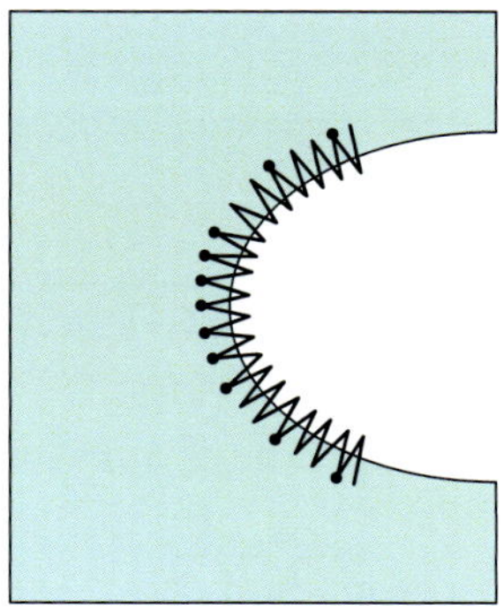

9. Do not backstitch at end of stitching. Pull threads to wrong side of background fabric; knot thread and trim ends.
10. Carefully tear away stabilizer.

QUILTING

Quilting holds the three layers (top, batting, and backing) of the quilt together and can be done by hand or machine. Because marking, layering, and quilting are interrelated and may be done in different orders depending on circumstances, please read entire ***Quilting*** *section, pages xxx-xxx, before beginning project.*

MARKING QUILTING LINES

Quilting lines may be marked using fabric marking pencils, chalk markers, or water- or air-soluble pens.

Simple quilting designs may be marked with chalk or chalk pencil after basting. A small area may be marked, then quilted, before moving to next area to be marked. Intricate designs should be marked before basting using a more durable marker.

Caution: Pressing may permanently set some marks. **Test** different markers **on scrap fabric** to find one that marks clearly and can be thoroughly removed.

A wide variety of pre-cut quilting stencils, as well as entire books of quilting patterns, are available. Using a stencil makes it easier to mark intricate or repetitive designs.

To make a stencil from a pattern, center template plastic over pattern and use a permanent marker to trace pattern onto plastic. Use a craft knife with single or double blade to cut channels along traced lines **(Fig. 19)**.

Fig. 19

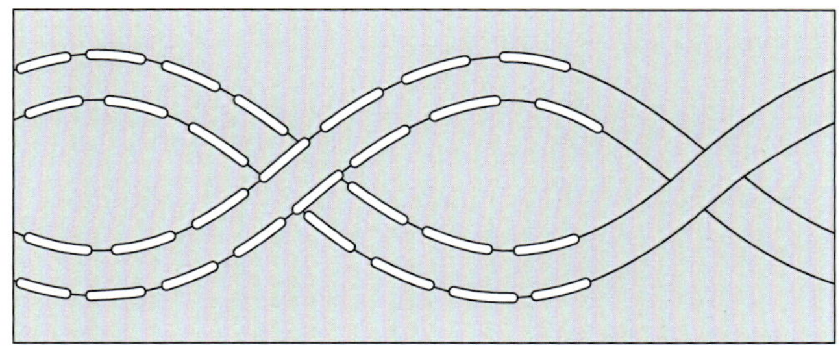

PREPARING THE BACKING

To allow for slight shifting of quilt top during quilting, backing should be approximately 4" larger on all sides. Yardage requirements listed for quilt backings are calculated for 43"/44"w fabric. Using 90"w or 108"w fabric for the backing of a bed-sized quilt may eliminate piecing. To piece a backing using 43"/44"w fabric, use the following instructions.

1. Measure length and width of quilt top; add 8" to each measurement.
2. If determined width is 79" or less, cut backing fabric into two lengths slightly longer than determined *length* measurement. Trim selvages. Place lengths with right sides facing and sew long edges together, forming tube **(Fig. 20)**. Match seams and press along one fold **(Fig. 21)**. Cut along pressed fold to form single piece **(Fig. 22)**.

Fig. 20

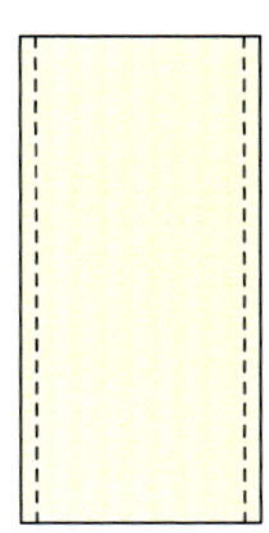

Fig. 21

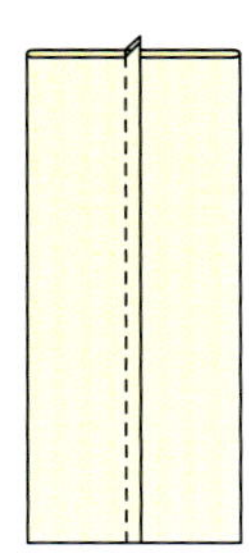

Fig. 22

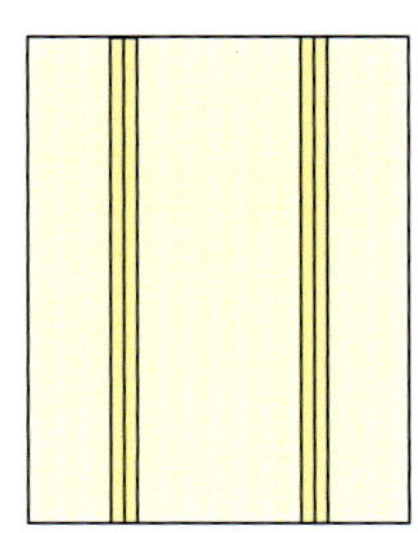

3. If determined width is more than 79", it may require less fabric yardage if the backing is pieced horizontally. Divide determined *length* measurement by 40" to determine how many widths will be needed. Cut required number of widths the determined *width* measurement. Trim selvages. Sew long edges together to form single piece.
4. Trim backing to size determined in Step 1; press seam allowances open.

CHOOSING THE BATTING

The appropriate batting will make quilting easier. For fine hand quilting, choose low-loft batting. All cotton or cotton/polyester blend battings work well for machine quilting because the cotton helps "grip" quilt layers. If quilt is to be tied, a high-loft batting, sometimes called extra-loft or fat batting, may be used to make quilt "fluffy."

Types of batting include cotton, polyester, wool, cotton/polyester blend, cotton/wool blend, and silk.

When selecting batting, refer to package labels for characteristics and care instructions. Cut batting same size as prepared backing.

ASSEMBLING THE QUILT

1. Examine wrong side of quilt top closely; trim any seam allowances and clip any threads that may show through front of the quilt. Press quilt top, being careful not to "set" any marked quilting lines.
2. Place backing *wrong* side up on flat surface. Use masking tape to tape edges of backing to surface. Place batting on top of backing fabric. Smooth batting gently, being careful not to stretch or tear. Center quilt top *right* side up on batting.
3. Use 1" rustproof safety pins to "pin-baste" all layers together, spacing pins approximately 4" apart. Begin at center and work toward outer edges to secure all layers. If possible, place pins away from areas that will be quilted, although pins may be removed as needed when quilting.

MACHINE QUILTING METHODS

Use general-purpose thread in bobbin. Do not use quilting thread. Thread the needle of machine with general-purpose thread or transparent monofilament thread to make quilting blend with quilt top fabrics. Use decorative thread, such as a metallic or contrasting-color general-purpose thread, to make quilting lines stand out more.

Straight-Line Quilting

The term "straight-line" is somewhat deceptive, since curves (especially gentle ones) as well as straight lines can be stitched with this technique.

1. Set stitch length for six to ten stitches per inch and attach walking foot to sewing machine.
2. Determine which section of quilt will have longest continuous quilting line, oftentimes area from center top to center bottom. Roll up and secure each edge of quilt to help reduce the bulk, keeping fabrics smooth. Smaller projects may not need to be rolled.
3. Begin stitching on longest quilting line, using very short stitches for the first 1/4" to "lock" quilting. Stitch across project, using one hand on each side of walking foot to slightly spread fabric and to guide fabric through machine. Lock stitches at end of quilting line.
4. Continue machine quilting, stitching longer quilting lines first to stabilize quilt before moving on to other areas.

Free-Motion Quilting

Free-motion quilting may be free form or may follow a marked pattern.

1. Attach darning foot to sewing machine and lower or cover feed dogs.
2. Position quilt under darning foot; lower foot. Holding top thread, take a stitch and pull bobbin thread to top of quilt. To "lock" beginning of quilting line, hold top and bobbin threads while making three to five stitches in place.
3. Use one hand on each side of darning foot to slightly spread fabric and to move fabric through the machine. Even stitch length is achieved by using smooth, flowing hand motion and steady machine speed. Slow machine speed and fast hand movement will create long stitches. Fast machine speed and slow hand movement will create short stitches. Move quilt sideways, back and forth, in a circular motion, or in a random motion to create desired designs; do not rotate quilt. Lock stitches at end of each quilting line.

MAKING A HANGING SLEEVE

Attaching a hanging sleeve to back of wall hanging or quilt before the binding is added allows project to be displayed on wall.

1. Measure width of quilt top edge and subtract 1". Cut piece of fabric 7"w by determined measurement.
2. Press short edges of fabric piece $^{1}/_{4}$" to wrong side; press edges $^{1}/_{4}$" to wrong side again and machine stitch in place.
3. Matching wrong sides, fold piece in half lengthwise to form tube.
4. Follow project instructions to sew binding to quilt top and to trim backing and batting. Before Blindstitching binding to backing, match raw edges and stitch hanging sleeve to center top edge on back of quilt.
5. Finish binding quilt, treating hanging sleeve as part of backing.
6. Blindstitch bottom of hanging sleeve to backing, taking care not to stitch through to front of quilt.

BINDING

MAKING STRAIGHT-GRAIN BINDING

1. To determine length of strip needed, measure edges of quilt and add 12".
2. Cut crosswise strips of binding fabric the determined length and the width called for in project instructions.
3. Using a diagonal seam **(Fig. 23)**, sew binding strips together end to end. Trim seam allowances to $^{1}/_{4}$". Press seam allowances open.

Fig. 23

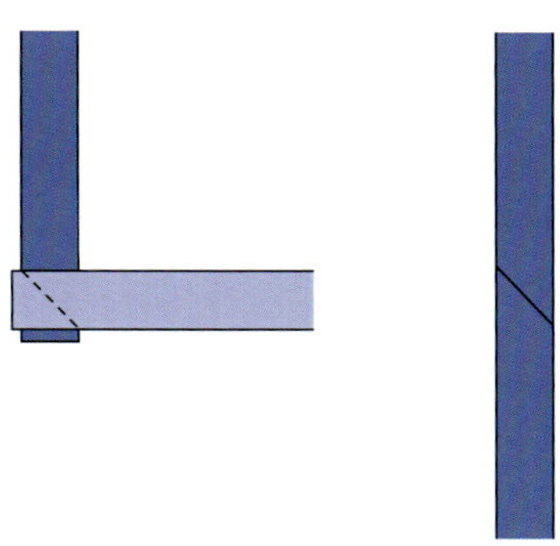

4. Matching wrong sides and raw edges, press strip(s) in half lengthwise to complete binding.

MAKING CONTINUOUS BIAS BINDING

1. Use square cut from binding fabric called for in project instructions. Cut square in half diagonally to make two triangles.
2. With right sides together and using a $^{1}/_{4}$" seam allowance, sew triangles together **(Fig. 24)**; press seam allowances open.

Fig. 24

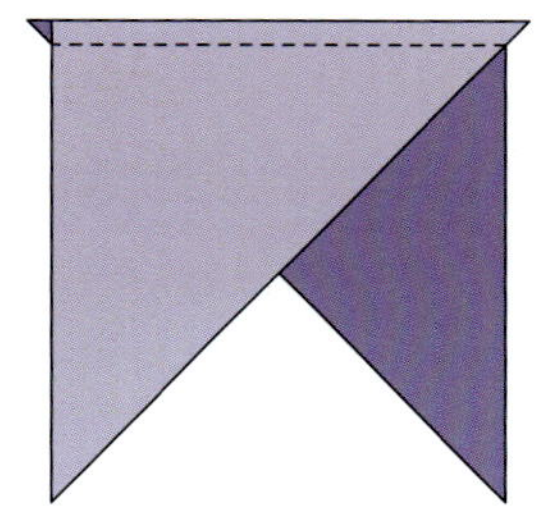

3. On wrong side of fabric, draw lines $2^{1}/_{2}$" apart **(Fig. 25)**. Cut off any remaining fabric less than this width.

Fig. 25

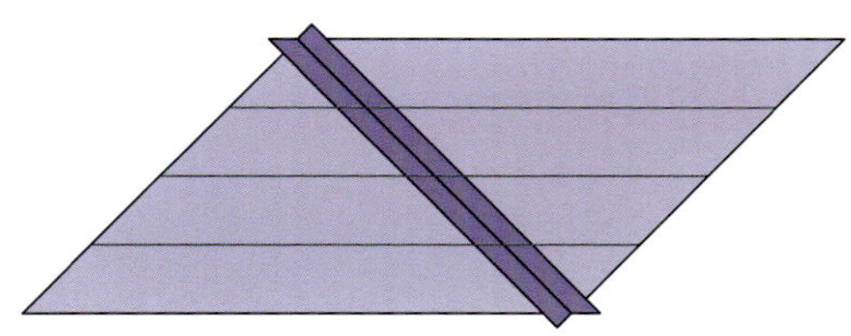

4. With right sides inside, bring short edges together to form a tube; match raw edges so that first drawn line of top section meets second drawn line of bottom section **(Fig. 26)**.

Fig. 26

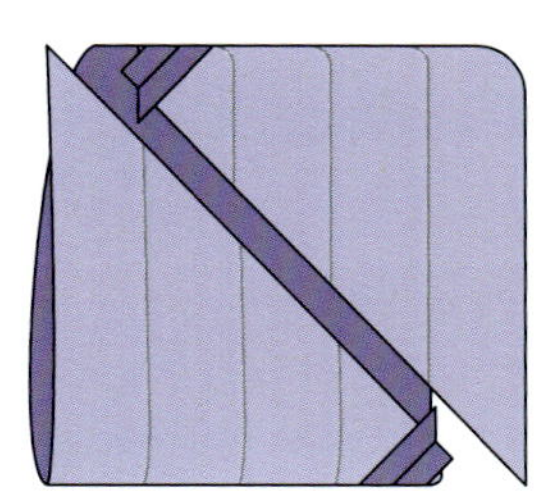

5. Carefully pin edges together by inserting pins through drawn lines at point where drawn lines intersect, making sure pins go through intersections on both sides. Using a 1/4" seam allowance, sew edges together; press seam allowances open.
6. To cut continuous strip, begin cutting along first drawn line **(Fig. 27)**. Continue cutting along drawn line around tube.

Fig. 27

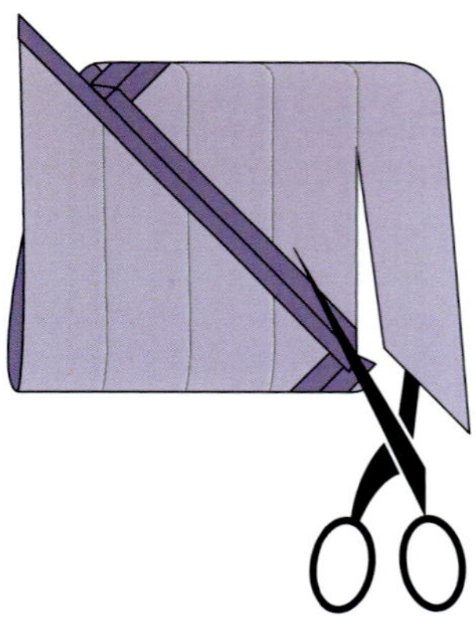

7. Trim ends of bias strip square.

ATTACHING BINDING WITH MITERED CORNERS

1. Beginning with one end near center on bottom edge of quilt, lay binding around quilt to make sure that seams in binding will not end up at a corner. Adjust placement if necessary. Matching raw edges of binding to raw edge of quilt top, pin binding to right side of quilt along one edge.
2. When you reach first corner, mark 1/4" from corner of quilt top **(Fig. 28)**.

Fig. 28

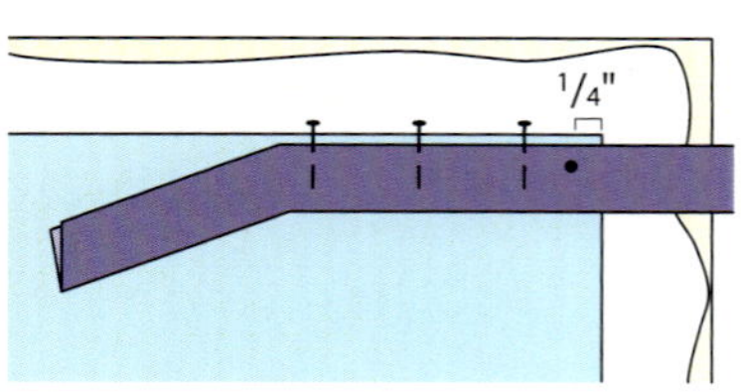

3. Beginning approximately 10" from end of binding and using 1/4" seam allowance, sew binding to quilt, backstitching at beginning of stitching and at mark **(Fig. 29)**. Lift needle out of fabric and clip thread.

Fig. 29

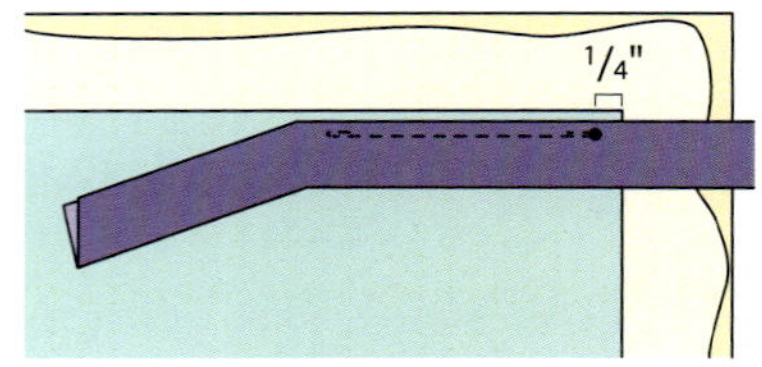

4. Fold binding as shown in **Figs. 30-31** and pin binding to adjacent side, matching raw edges. When you've reached the next corner, mark 1/4" from edge of quilt top.

Fig. 30

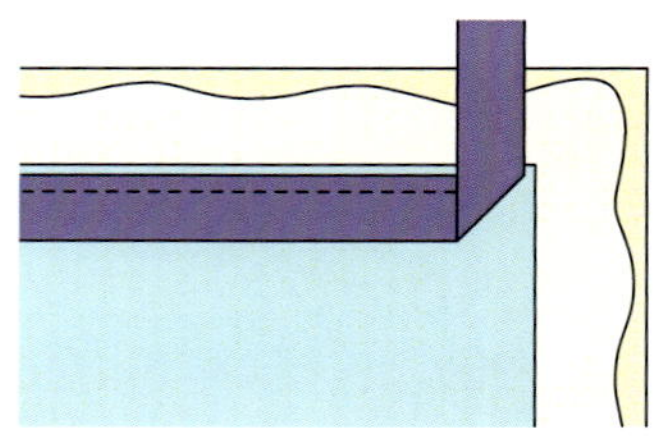

Fig. 31

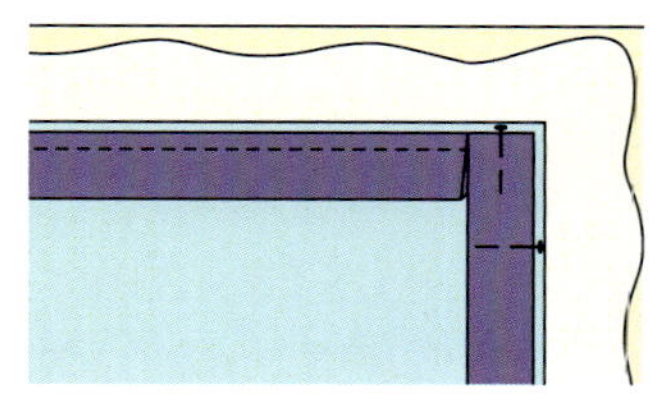

5. Backstitching at edge of quilt top, sew pinned binding to quilt **(Fig. 32)**; backstitch at the next mark. Lift needle out of fabric and clip thread.

Fig. 32

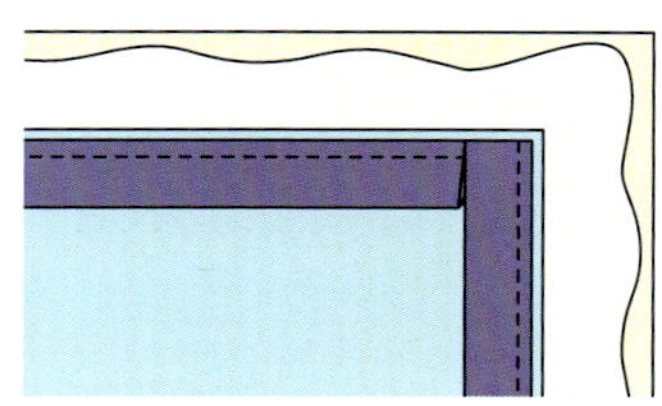

6. Continue sewing binding to quilt, stopping approximately 10" from starting point **(Fig. 33)**.

Fig. 33

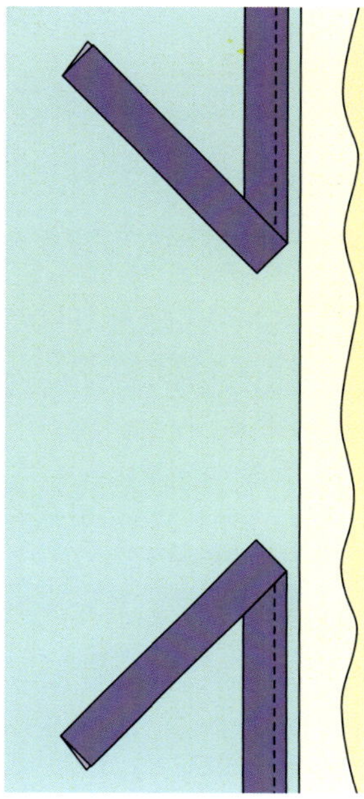

7. Bring beginning and end of binding to center of opening and fold each end back, leaving a 1/4" space between folds **(Fig. 34)**. Finger press folds.

Fig. 34

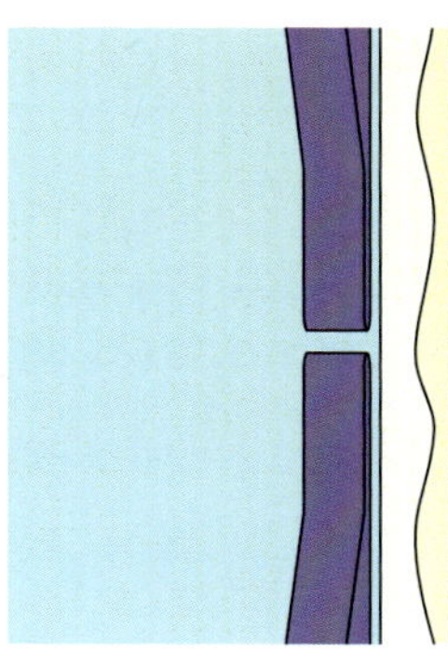

8. Unfold ends of binding and draw a line across wrong side in finger-pressed crease. Draw a line through the lengthwise pressed fold of binding at the same spot to create a cross mark. With edge of ruler at cross mark, line up 45° angle marking on ruler with one long side of binding. Draw a diagonal line from edge to edge. Repeat on remaining end, making sure that the two diagonal lines are angled the same way **(Fig. 35)**.

Fig. 35

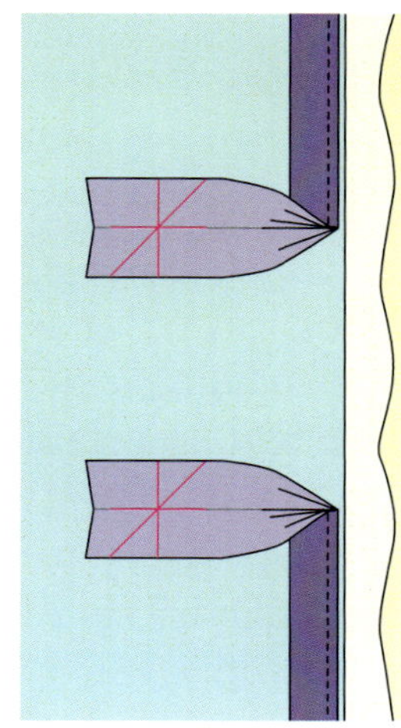

9. Matching right sides and diagonal lines, pin binding ends together at right angles **(Fig. 36)**.

Fig. 36

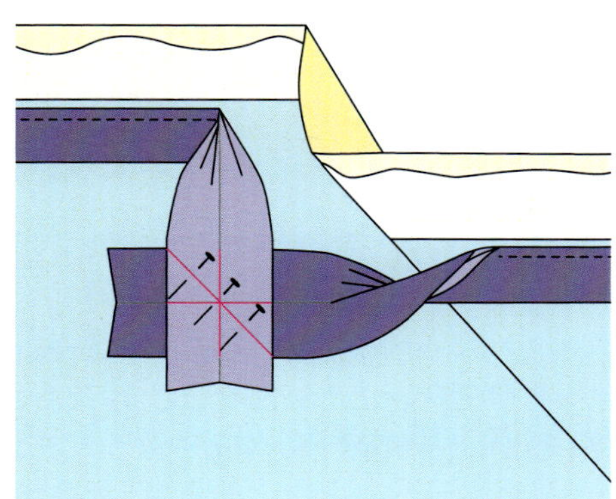

10. Machine stitch along diagonal line **(Fig. 37)**, removing pins as you stitch.

Fig. 37

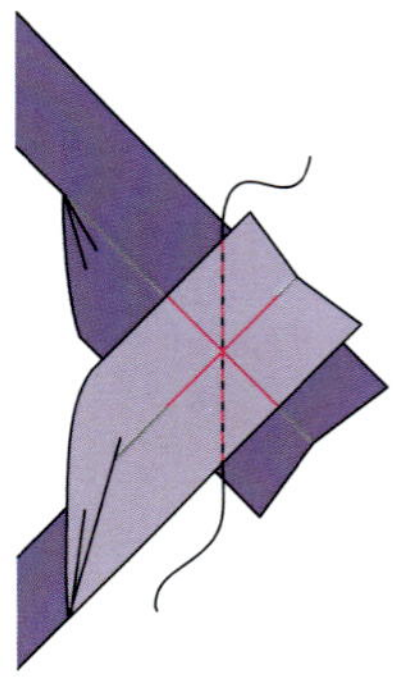

11. Lay binding against quilt to double check that it is correct length.
12. Trim binding ends, leaving $^1/_4$" seam allowance; press seam open. Stitch binding to quilt.
13. Trim backing and batting a scant $^1/_4$" larger than quilt top so that batting and backing will fill the binding when it is folded over to quilt backing. If using narrower binding, trim backing and batting even with edges of quilt top.
14. On one edge of quilt, fold binding over to quilt backing and pin pressed edge in place, covering stitching line ***(Fig. 38)***. On adjacent side, fold binding over, forming a mitered corner ***(Fig. 39)***. Repeat to pin remainder of binding in place.

Fig. 38

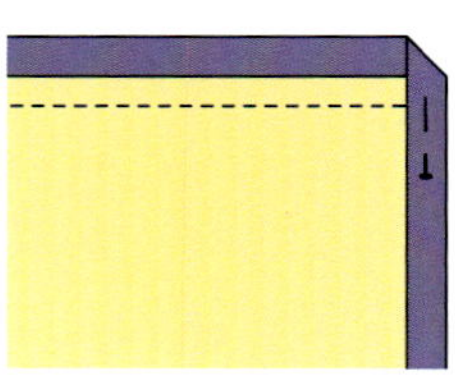

Fig. 39

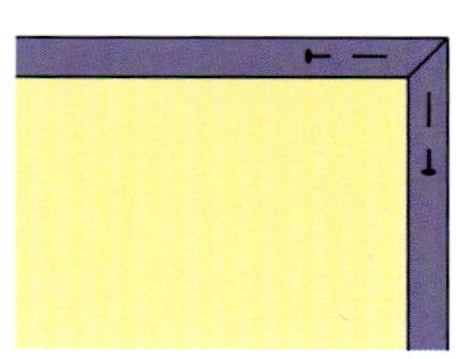

15. Blindstitch binding to backing, taking care not to stitch through to front of quilt.

Go to bit.ly/7363-A-Star-is-Born to get instructions for this adorable quilt.

Susan would like to thank machine quilters, Melanie Leckie (www.ohsewloved.blogspot.com) and The Longarm Network (www.thelongarmnetwork.com) for their beautiful quilting on some of the quilts in this book.

Made in U.S.A.

Production Team: Technical Editor – Lisa Lancaster; Senior Graphic Artist – Lora Puls, Graphic Artist – Kytanna McFarlin, Photography Stylist – Lori Wenger; Photographer – Jason Masters